The Echoes We Make

A Men's Appreciation Anthology
by Various Authors

Compiled by Quillkeepers Press

QUILLKEEPERS PRESS

Dear Reader,

The Echoes We Make is a powerful, tender, and expansive literary tribute to men and the enduring impact of their presence in our lives. Across cultures, generations, and lived experiences, this anthology gathers 47 global voices: 35 poets and 12 essayists, memoirists, and short-story writers, who collectively bear witness to the ways men shape, guide, protect, teach, love, and leave their marks on the world.

Rather than offering a singular definition of masculinity, *The Echoes We Make* embraces its many expressions. Within these pages, men appear as lovers and partners, coaches and mentors, fathers, stepfathers, grandfathers, caregivers, teachers, leaders, friends, and quiet guardians. Some are heroic in moments of sacrifice; others, in everyday consistency; some are loud in their devotion; others, remembered for the stillness of their presence. Together, these narratives form a chorus that honors not perfection, but humanity.

The anthology moves fluidly between intimate personal remembrance and broader cultural reflection. Readers encounter wartime leadership expressed not through rank, but through quiet service; ancestral strength passed down through storytelling and labor; fathers who give everything they have so future generations may thrive; mentors who redirect lives through patience and belief; and men whose moral compasses steady entire communities. These stories span continents and traditions, revealing how care, responsibility, courage, and integrity transcend borders.

Poetry throughout the collection captures the emotional undercurrents of male influence, of grief carried silently, of love expressed through action, of pride inherited and earned, and of the ache of absence when a guiding figure is lost. Essays and memoirs expand this emotional landscape, offering reflections on boyhood, fatherhood, friendship, legacy, and the evolving role of men in families and societies. Short fiction weaves myth, memory, and imagination, reminding us that the echoes men leave behind are not always linear, but are no less profound.

Importantly, *The Echoes We Make* does not shy away from complexity. It acknowledges struggle, vulnerability, contradiction, and growth. It recognizes that many men lead without recognition, love without language, and sacrifice without applause. In doing so, the collection creates space for gratitude, spoken and unspoken, toward those who showed up when it mattered most.

At its heart, this collection is an act of collective appreciation. It is a book of thanks for the men who raised us, the men who stood beside us, the men who taught us how to endure, and the men whose lessons continue long after they are gone. It asks readers to listen closely to what remains after a voice falls silent, after footsteps fade, after a life has been lived with intention.

This anthology will resonate with readers seeking connection, reflection, and recognition of the men who have shaped their lives. It is both a celebration and a remembrance, offering a lasting testament to the echoes men leave behind—not only in families and communities, but in the hearts of those who carry their influence forward.

Essays, Memoirs, Short Stories

Biographies,
Essays, Memoirs,
Short Stories

Jeffrey Beck is a retired Army soldier and a graduate student in the MFA program at Southern New Hampshire University. He earned his BA in English, summa cum laude, from American Military University. He lives with his wife on a five-acre homestead in southern Virginia, where he enjoys tending chickens, reading, and writing fiction, fantasy, and poetry. He is currently working on a memoir about his combat experience in Iraq. Jeffrey published *Letters to My Homestead*, a poetry collection, in September 2025 and has been published

on poetry websites and in anthologies for
Quillkeepers Press and *Perserverance & Resilience*,
a veterans' poetry anthology. Connect with Jeffrey on
Instagram at <u>j.b._leroy.writer</u>

Christmas at O.P. 445

I have lost count of the Christmas mornings I've woken up to whispers and crinkling wrapping paper; the hymn of cinnamon rolls baking in the kitchen, the aroma drifting through the house. Christmas Eve was reserved for my maternal grandparents' holiday gathering. The entire family—patriarch and matriarch, six girls, their spouses, and seventeen grandchildren— boisterous, breaking bread and filling plates with homemade favorites. These core memories were created during childhood and remained a tradition for a little over two decades.

On Christmas morning 2005, I awoke in Ramadi, Iraq. The War was in its second year, and we had been there for five months; I was 23. My alarm had betrayed me that morning, and the early hours slipped past me, unnoticed. I was set to wake at two a.m. so that I could call home. The East Coast of the United States would still be celebrating Christmas Eve. By the time my combat boots hit the powdery sand, I was behind and rushing; it was closer to four. The others, ghostly figures in the early morning fog and dust, were loading their bags into the gun-trucks and gathering for the convoy briefing. This routine mission felt like anything but on this special morning. I felt off. I missed home, I missed my family, and all I wanted was the full plate, holiday music, and cousins.

At five, we rolled out of the main gate, headed to a pinprick of an outpost, twenty miles east toward Fallujah. The dim sky remained colorless as we drove over rough pavement. Shuttered houses were still while stray dogs huddled for warmth around pancaked buildings. Nothing moved but us in our heavily armored trucks.

Once we arrived and the team we were relieving cleared out, I began my shift, somber and resigned, knowing I'd be spending Christmas in a cold watchtower and taking periodic slumbers in the half-buried, dirty Conex box we called home every third day. We'd rotate shifts in a freezing steel-plated tower until six the following morning.

Our detail-oriented mission was simple but distinct: three teams of six, rotated every 24 hours, each with two communications specialists, two medics, and two recovery/mechanics. We were stationed there in case a passing combat patrol or allied convoy needed assistance or a safe place to regroup. Other than our personal bag, we had next to nothing except ammunition, a small ration of food, and bottles of mineral water warmed by the daytime desert heat that sat by the door. Hesco barriers, which were five-foot-square wire cages lined with fabric and filled with sand, surrounded us, shielding us from the outside world and offering quasi-protection from rocket or mortar blasts.

I distinctly remember this morning feeling different. It was a low point for me and the rest of us. I had been away for almost a year by this point and still had six months to go. With it being Christmas and us being so far from our families, our daily routine, and our regular lives, this day was the lowest I had ever felt. For some, it was the first holiday away from loved ones. For others, just another long, lonely milestone in the desert, another check on the list of missed life events, collateral damage from a career in the service. Even the desert seemed more subdued than usual.

Around five p.m., halfway through our mission, I spotted an American convoy approaching from the west. The radio crackled with a familiar call sign: "OP445, this is *Hammer Seven*, approaching your location, over." Visitors? That was unexpected. A couple of five-ton trucks and escort gun-trucks pulled off the highway and crossed the sand berm. And there, bobbing above the gun turrets, were bright red reindeer antlers strapped to the helmets of grinning gunners.

The armored trucks parked behind the Hescos blocked my view. I moved to the southern side of the tower and peered out. Our Commanding Officer—*Hammer Six*, and First Sergeant—*Hammer Seven* appeared from below. They small-talked with us, complimented the cleanliness of the tower, inspected the fifty-caliber machine gun, and looked out over the sandy expanse we watched day and night. Minutes later, two more soldiers climbed the ladder, and the commander told my counterpart and me to head down to the stockade and grab some chow.

When I stepped into the corral below, I halted, astonished. About twenty of the Battalion's Company leadership, platoon sergeants, and key staff and drivers from my home company stood gathered around two tables loaded with portable, steaming food totes. The chow hall not only provided a holiday meal for base personnel but also prepared meals for the remote observation posts scattered throughout the countryside. The meal was ham and turkey slices, buttered corn, stuffing, and mashed potatoes with gravy—all still hot. The staff served the six of us first, then joined us with their own overflowing plates. We sat wherever we could: on cots, ammo crates, or cross-legged on the ground. We ate together, trading stories and laughter from lives that felt so far away.

We smiled and cracked jokes, but there was a residual ache behind our eyes. We were thousands of miles from the twinkling-colored lights, the chaos of tearing into paper-wrapped gifts, familiar voices, and the warmth of family dinners. And yet, at that moment, with plates of turkey and mashed potatoes balanced on our knees, and the desert wind howling in the distance, tiny grains of sand crunching in my teeth felt like family. This wasn't home, but the effort from leadership reminded me that we were seen and that we mattered. For a few precious minutes, the loneliness and solitude of war were softened by a hot meal and genuine connection. We weren't *just* hardened soldiers—warriors, but fragile mortals clinging to childhood memories and tradition, each trying to make sense of a holiday that looked nothing like the ones we remembered.

Twenty minutes later, they packed up the food and left for the next location, except for our Commanding Officer, Captain Neilson. He returned to the tower, climbed the ladder, and relieved the lowest-ranking soldier on duty, without announcement or ceremony. When the relieved soldier returned to the safe corral, he shrugged, "He told me to go get some rest."

When the next pair was to report, my Commander called on the wired rotary field phone and instructed the lowest ranking of the duo to stay down in the sleeping quarters—he would be covering the shift. That night, my company commander stood post for twelve hours, covering one shift for each of the six of us.

This act on Christmas wasn't merely a kind gesture: it was leadership in its purest, quietest form. There was no fanfare, no orders, and no recognition. Just a man stepping into the December cold, on the darkest of nights, simply so the others could rest. His climbing into that lonely tower changed something inside of me. I saw what true leadership is and how simple acts can be infectious. That night, he wasn't a distant voice of an authoritative silhouette behind the orders we followed. He spoke few words, but his presence said everything. I carry the image of a man standing under the stars in the cool desert night, no sleep, no breaks, just a humble act that allowed six lower-enlisted to get a little extra rest on Christmas at war.

Now, two decades later, every time I pile my Christmas plate high with turkey, ham, mashed potatoes, and gravy, I consider this an act of selfless leadership and how it was more clear than any medal, speech, or commendation could ever be. I think about what it meant to be seen, to have served and be served, and to be honorably led.

Andrew L. Huerta lives in Tucson, Arizona, where he has spent the last twenty-seven years in Higher Education, teaching/advising students who are the first in their families to attend college. With his MA in Creative Writing and PhD in Education, his collection of short stories entitled *A Different Man* was published in 2021 by Bold Stroke Books (an independent publisher), and he is now looking to publish his first novel, *Raggedy Anthony*. His short stories have appeared in *Chelsea Station Magazine*, *The Round Up Writer's Zine: Pride Edition*, *Jonathan*, *The Storyteller*, and the anthologies *Queerly Loving, First Came Fear: New Tales of*

Horror, and *Hashtag Queer Volume 2*. His personal essays have appeared in *Fashionably Late: Gay, Bi, and Trans Men Who Came Out Later in Life*, *Queer Families: An LGBTQ+ True Stories Anthology*, and, of course, Quillkeepers Press' *The Heart of Pride Volume II*.

Cuco's Story

My Tata, Refugio Martinez Huerta, aka Cuco, was always referred to as a man's man. At 5 feet 7 inches tall and weighing 150 pounds, he was stout, tough, and solid. A man who worked hard to support his family, and one who'd never let anyone push him around. There are many stories I can share about my tata, but my father used to tell us the story of *Tata the Boxer.* Dad would vividly describe how Tata loved to share many of his life stories. Dad, like my tata, would excitedly act out the drama as the story unfolded. Imitating Tata, Dad would stand in front of us, his five children seated together on our living room couch, and we'd listen intently. With his fists in the air, he'd show us how Tata would box, and he'd dramatize as much of the story as he could. In a loud, booming voice, Dad would proudly share the story of *Tata the Boxer*. And he'd always emphasize how Tata became one of the most admired men at the roundhouse in Tucson, where Tata worked as a boilermaker for the Southern Pacific Railroad.

My father would start his story by reminding us, "When Cuco was younger, he was an amateur boxer. He trained in El Paso when he was a teenager and first came to the United States. And then, he trained at a gym in Los Angeles when he first started working for the Southern Pacific Railroad." Standing in our living room, in Southern Arizona, Dad would always point east toward Texas, then west toward California. "And then, in 1932, when Cuco received his final assignment, here in the roundhouse in Tucson, which used to be located downtown, just by the Cathedral, he stopped boxing. With a growing family, Cuco tried to focus on work, but soon enough, started fighting again when the Tucson roundhouse started its Friday night fights."

"You see," Dad would say. "After work on Fridays, the employees would gather at a certain area just outside the roundhouse It was the sanctioned place for the Friday night fights, and the fights would take place between the roundhouse employees. Those larger, stronger employees, who were brave enough to sign up to fight." Dad would pause and hold up his hands. "And in those days, at the Friday night fights, no gloves were used. The fighters would just box with their bare knuckles." Dad would close his hands and show us his clenched fists. "Of course, most of the employees and the upper management would watch. Bets would be made, and every now and then, there'd be a referee. They'd get a referee for some of the bigger fights. Just to try and keep the fighters honest and safe."

"And, of course, due to the limited number of employees who would sign up to fight, there'd be no strict rules, and definitely no recognized weight classifications. So, while the fights were a bit of a free-for-all, and the matches were never officially endorsed, the management of the roundhouse saw them as harmless, fun, and good for employee morale."

"So, for Cuco, it didn't take long for him to become one of the favorite boxers at the Friday night fights." Dad would stop and shake his finger *NO* in front of us, attempting to emphasize his point. "And no one, no other employee within 20 pounds, could stand up to Cuco, and his pounding. And he quickly emerged as the Mexican champion of the Friday night fights."

"Now," Dad would begin again and place his hands behind his back. "The fight Cuco was most proud of was when he came up against this first-generation Italian boxer. He was just hired at the roundhouse, and he spoke only broken English and no Spanish. At 5 feet 10 inches and weighing 170 pounds, the Italian was taller and heavier than Cuco. And as The Italian began to box more and more during the Friday night fights, he became known as *'the-great-white-hope'* to all of the other Anglo-American employees, especially those who worked in management."

"And it was just a matter of time before the employees began clamoring for a showdown between Cuco and The Italian. And Cuco was anxious to take on the big fighter and show off for his friends. And the confident, cocky Italian, never saw Cuco as much competition. So, Cuco agreed to the fight, and The Italian agreed too, and the fight was set for the next payday, about two weeks away. All of the Mexican employees saw the match as a fight between "La Raza and Los Gringos" and, of course, all of the other employees, especially the management, began to support The Italian."

Here, Dad would usually pause and hold up his hands, attempting to emphasize the drama. "Now, the buildup to the fight caused plenty of excitement around the roundhouse. Sides were taken. The wagering, or the betting on which boxer would win, increased more and more as the date approached. And when Friday night came around, and the 5 o'clock whistle blew, a huge crowd had gathered around the fighting area."

"You see, outside the roundhouse, there was no formal boxing ring. No ropes closed off the boxing area. And no corner men would help, or even coach the boxers. Instead, it was an open area, with three sides where the spectators could stand and watch the fights." Enamored by Dad's story, all five of us would lean forward in our seats. We'd watch Dad as he paced off a small area in the middle of our living room, trying to show us the shape of the boxing area. "And, on the fourth side," he'd add. "There was the supply pile with rows of machine parts, lumber, steel rods, and the creosote-treated logs that were used as rail beds." Dad would then attempt to show us the height of the supply pile and how it dominated the one side. "Now, on that Friday night, they weren't the only fighters to fight, so after the preliminary rounds, they announced the big event. And they had formal introductions, where the two fighters, Cuco and The Italian, were brought to the center, and told to shake hands."

"And the referee, who was brought in special that night, announced that it was to be a 10-round fight, with 3-minute rounds, and the rounds would be marked by the clanging of an iron triangle, held by someone who stood in the corner. Someone in management who had a good watch."

"So, when the triangle first sounded, Cuco approached the center of the ring and took a good look at his opponent." Dad would hold his fists up in front of him, trying to mimic a boxer, and even wipe his nose with his thumb every now and then. "The Italian, he was a tall, sculpted man, with broad shoulders and long, muscular arms. Unlike the Mexican employees, the Italian was light-skinned, almost pale, but still had jet-black, curly hair. And Cuco could see a smile, a bit of a smirk on The Italian's face. The Italian thought it would be an easy fight. And all Cuco could think about was knocking that smirk off of his face."

"The two at first circled each other cautiously, trying to feel each other out." Dad, with his fists still up in front of him, would bounce up and down on the balls of his feet. "Cuco started to dance around him, looking for an opening, and soon figured that he'd have to get under those arms, try to avoid The Italian's long reach, and keep himself at a safe distance. Cuco, knowing he had to find a weakness, started to jab and dance, jab and dance." Dad would keep bouncing up and down. "And with The Italian's initial swings, which were quick and clumsy, Cuco knew he wasn't a boxer; he was a street fighter, meaning that his swings were gonna remain wild, and all The Italian was looking for was a quick knockout."

"So, Cuco made a few adjustments and began waiting patiently for those periods of long, flailing, clumsy swings. And when they came, Cuco would counter with good, solid blows to the body." Dad would attempt to show us where The Italian would be in front of him, and then show us how Cuco would punch his opponent's body, mainly the kidneys and stomach. "Now, The Italian was able to land one or two good punches to Cuco's face, throwing him a bit off balance, and drawing blood from his mouth.

Surprised by the strength of each punch, Cuco realized that he was not going to be able to absorb too many of those blows. And by the end of the first round, Cuco had managed to land several blows to The Italian's chest and stomach."

"In the second round, The Italian was over his initial excitement, and he became more conscious of landing the one or two punches he needed for a quick knockout. But Cuco, with his training and conditioning, stayed on his toes, kept dancing, bobbing and weaving, a safe distance from The Italian. But The Italian had already landed several blows to Cuco's face, and blood was continuing to flow from his mouth." Dad would push out his bottom lip and look as sad as possible. "Still, Cuco stayed focused and was finding it easier to land the body blows he needed to wear down his opponent. And Cuco could see The Italian wince, and let out a loud moan with each and every blow.

The Italian's long, muscled arms were getting heavy; he was getting tired, and his arms were coming down to better defend his stomach. When the triangle rang, Cuco stepped over to his corner, confident that he would now be able to reach The Italian's face."

"In round three, The Italian became even more tired and reckless. Cuco's body blows were taking their toll on the big man, and he was beginning to wrap his arms around Cuco. He'd hang on Cuco, trying to hold himself up, not once, but several times that round. And Cuco, sensing his opening, began to yell at the man." Dad would pause and hold one finger over his lips, trying to watch his words. "Now, I can't tell you what Cuco called The Italian. Those are not nice words, even if they were in Spanish, and The Italian probably didn't understand what he was saying. But Cuco was angry and wanted The Italian to back off. And the referee was also yelling at The Italian to step back. The ref would force himself between the two fighters, pulling them apart."

"And soon, the crowd joined in yelling, and booing, and whistling at The Italian. And as soon as The Italian stepped back, Cuco attacked, pummeling him in the face." Dad again would bob and weave, doing his best to show us Cuco's aggression. "The Italian's chest was now bright red from all the blows, and his face was a bloody mess. He was exhausted, angry, and frustrated. And when that round ended, The Italian did not step away to his corner. Instead, he turned toward the supply pile, stumbled over, and picked up a piece of lumber, like a 2x4 wooden plank, probably about 4 feet long. As he turned, stepped to the center of the ring, and raised the 2x4 in the air, Cuco automatically raised his arm to cover his face." Dad would step in front of us again and raise his imaginary weapon over our heads. "When the blow landed, it hit Cuco's right shoulder and sent him sprawling down into the dirt." Dad would again lower his arms and place one finger over his mouth. "And a hush came over the crowd," he'd whisper. "Men at the front of the crowds had to raise their arms and hold everyone back, preventing some of the other men from rushing in. Stunned, Cuco steadied himself, rolled into a sitting position, and held his injured shoulder. His face turned from shock to rage, and he locked eyes with The Italian." Dad would stare at us intently.

"With his left hand, Cuco pushed himself to his feet, walked over to the supply pile, and grabbed a 3-foot steel rod, the kind of rod they used to reinforce cement. He was angry, in pain, and ready to kill The Italian. But when The Italian realized what he had done, he dropped the 2x4, fell to his knees, clasped his hands, and started yelling, 'Scusa! Sono Spiacente', 'Sorry. I'm sorry'. Still on his knees in front of Cuco, he covered his face in shame and continued to cry and cry. And Cuco, watching the man cower in front of him, walked over to the crying Italian, still with his hands tightly wrapped around the rod. He stood over The Italian for a moment and dropped the rod. With his hand still on his injured shoulder, Cuco walked over to the 2x4 and kicked it away. Stepping back over his opponent, Cuco lowered his hand and, with a slight tap, pushed The Italian onto his back. The Italian then rolled over on his side, curled himself into a ball, and continued to cry. And that was it. The Italian was down, and the fight was over."

"As soon as Cuco gently pushed The Italian backward, the crowd went wild.

They yelled and screamed for Cuco; they celebrated his victory, and soon enough, all wagers were paid. The crowd had come hoping to see blood and guts, and almost witnessed a killing. But they celebrated Cuco, who'd won the fight, fair and square. And your Tata, the boxer, became the undisputed champion of the Tucson roundhouse Friday night fights." Dad would clasp his hands together in front of him, lift them up over his shoulders, and shake them vigorously, moving from one shoulder to the other. "Now," Dad would finally say. "Let's get some lunch and see if the football game is on yet."

That was one of Dad's favorite stories about his father. He loved sharing with us what he could about Tata's strength and bravery. And Dad would always emphasize how hard his father fought to make his way in this country and provide for his family as much as he could, in any way possible.

Marc Hequet lives in St. Paul, Minnesota, USA.

Bez Laterals the Baby to Bulfinch

Is it true that men buttress reality with make-believe worlds of their own? And the highest and noblest functions of their minds cooperate in this?

If so, then this narrative is about irrational throes and how to escape them. A narrative on how *not* to have irrational throes in the first place makes better advice, but a poor story.

Irrational throes? In this case, it concerns an otherwise competent adult male and how he manages during one such throe: having a baby.

Does any man ever face a steeper climb? We'll call him Bulfinch.

First, pagan gods: Pagan gods, as you know, were ubiquitous in antiquity and are long since demoted to mere demons by devout Christian cleansing. Evil demons, one would think.

Yet here, there, everywhere in excavations around the Mediterranean Sea, archaeologists and tomb raiders and relic snatchers find amulets of one such deity-demon whose influence perhaps survives even to this day – actual influence, and for the good.

He's ugly. Rude. Ill-suited at childbed. Yet this is what Bez does: labor and delivery.

Scholars spell him *Bes,* but let's make it *Bez* so it doesn't look like a typo. Ancients weren't fussy about fricatives. Any sibilant will do. Ibiza, a resort island off Spain's east coast, is Bez's island, so named by Phoenician traders, counting on his goodwill. You can still sign up for a party cruise there, with unlimited drinks, lunch, and a deejay – all in keeping with the ways of Bez. Indeed, on any given cruise, he may be along just for the party.

Bez himself may come from Nubia, the land of Punt, or from Somalia or Ethiopia. He honks, and grunts, and rattles, and dances down the Nile before the pyramids go up. He builds quite a following among women, who just then are having babies hand over fist in the abundant tillage of the Nile valley. We find his amulets in mounting numbers up to the time of Cleopatra and thereafter, well into the Christian era.

You still see images of Bez here and there – bookshelf statuettes pillaged or copied, charms hanging on pretty throats. Bez, malformed bandyleg demon of antiquity, seems busy as ever on the blurry border cloaking reality from everything else.

He's the rock-and-roll racket at the wedding dance, then the security guard. Evil spirits swoop over the bouncing consummation of the bridal suite spot Bez and swoop out again. "Ooops!" they say. "This room is taken!" And they go curse something else.

Then Bez tends the bride in childbirth and guards the children as they grow. Bez tags along in the streets, scooping toddlers from under Roman chariots and oxcarts and, nowadays, from screeching tires where damn fools still drive too fast.

This makes Bez an angel, right? Rethink angels, then. He's a bowlegged bantamweight with oversize ears and obtrusive genitalia hanging right out in front of God and everybody else. Ancient Egyptian images routinely show other figures in dignified profile. Not Bez. He stares you down. And sticks out his tongue. Goggle eyes, feathers, a bushy tail, and no pants. Song, dance, and funny faces. How better to lighten a woman's childbed travail?

Or a man's. Men know nothing of childbirth. What other labor is like it? Plumbing? Wiring? Either can blow a man across the room and kill him. But it's not the same.

People love Bez. He can't be just gone, *poof*, period. He must still be on call when people need him, as with Bulfinch. So Bez and Bulfinch meet. Almost.

Let's get back to Bulfinch — Leopold Lexington "Stack" Bulfinch, "Stack" not for his height but for how he's put together. Come to think of it, Bulfinch resembles Bez. Bulfinch is top-heavy and walks funny. Kind of a lurching amble. Ten-year-old girls giggle behind his back. He's got a cute bottom, like a baby.

And remarkable agility. Classmates remember him playing leapfrog over parking meters. On the high-school football team, his career highlight is snatching a desperate lateral and bowlegging sixty yards to win the game.

Thus, Bulfinch is like any other young man: carefree, omniscient, quick with clumsy wit, quicker still in strategic retreat or outright flight. Terrified of women but clever among them – he supposes – deftly fending them away yet ever alert for new flowerbeds to plow.

Indeed, here and there beckons that fatal up-from-under look, blink-blink. Sometimes a woman wants him. Sometimes she gets what she wants. In this latest case, it's marriage. And a baby. And it's time.

Women who find themselves on this precarious cusp, among the ancients and to this day, appeal to any help available — to Eileithyia, to Hymen, Shasti, to the Blessed Virgin Mary — to any of many who assist women through this most miraculous and dangerous of days. Followers of Eileithyia indulge in the mysteries of Kore and Demeter, antediluvian goddesses. Eileithyia, spelled in loose Greek, bears some relation to the 'Elysian,' as in the Elysian Fields, where good ancients go when they die. Half a globe distant, Aztec women have the same privilege. Those who die in childbirth are esteemed as warriors and receive warriors' honors in the great beyond.

Having babies is a fight, all right. Sometimes, the baby stands its ground, which is the case with Bulfinch's pending progeny. Bulfinch, the nerve-wracked perpetrator, manfully endures about twenty hours of nothing happening except birth pangs, pushing, and swear words no mother should utter.

So *this*, Bulfinch marvels in exhausted desperation, *this* is man's highest calling. Making babies. For men, brief ecstasy that soon enough buries her in immense suffering, she whom he presumably loves. At this ogreous inference, fatigued to delirium, frantic for any succor, Bulfinch flees down hospital halls into the sun and air.

Bez, meanwhile, himself an ungulate, closer to pig than to any other animal, likewise is taking his ease in the open air and sunshine, among other ungulates. Just now, he reposes among the cows in the Elysian Fields, in pasturage assigned to lesser spirits.

The cows, however, are restless, unquiet. Perhaps one of their own is calving. Or something worse. Sensing vexatious tidings, cows rise from their own repose, accelerating to an actual trot back to their *kraal*. For all they know, Akyet raiders may be coming again to steal livestock. This entails no end of trouble for cows.

Such are the bothers that rouse Bez from his ease. Bez rouses.

Back outside the hospital, Bulfinch breaks into a run and staggers around a corner, where a food truck simmers, a *mariachi* band plays, and dancers whirl in a hip-thrusty *jarabe*. Abruptly, Bez is here as well. Heat, meat, and riotous rhythms always draw Bez even from the blessed abodes of the lesser spirits. It may be an animal sacrifice! To him! Thus, he is bound by the rules of spirithood to appear.

And here he is. A great dancer. You should see his *zapateado* atop the food truck, with a one-and-a-half gainer to the ground, then a real leg-waver of a headspin.

So we enter the blurred terminus separating the spirit world from the world of the street. And they meet, Bulfinch and Bez. As we say, almost.

It must happen like this: Bez dimly discerns a frenzied summons from something called a Bulfinch. Yet Bez himself is frenzied, as usual, in dance and merriment.

Meanwhile, fresh air and noise restore Bulfinch to his senses. He hurries back into the hospital. Bez sees and pursues.

To the task, then. Bez dances through glass doors, along corridors, and finds this Bulfinch taut as a lyre string in a dim room among creatures in masks, close-fitting hats, and full-length gowns. A baby squawls. Bez is too late!

He begins merrymaking anyway, sloshing Bulfinch with adrenaline, rousing him from the stupor of exhaustion.

A nurse cradles the wet thing, towels it, lays it gently in a warm bassinette, and returns to help clean up the mother.

Bez rattles over to this bassinette and snatches the new thing, hoists it up and down, up and down. He dances toward Bulfinch, up, down, up, down. Then he shovels the baby into the new father's arms.

That's all. Bez surveys the delivery room, sees everything in good hands, shakes his rattle, and dances out the door.

For the ensuing eternity, Bulfinch stares into the newborn's open, astonished eyes. The nurse, done tending the mother, turns again to the bassinet.

"Aighh!" she shrieks. "Where's the baby!?!"

Bulfinch delicately holds it out for her. She takes it with relief.

Indeed, the baby resembles Bez, enough just now that we may wonder at its paternity. The newcomer looks like a prune. But ugly. It soon sticks out its tongue.

So, we see, irrational throes ever threaten to propel us right over the edge, but needn't. Bring to bear your mental prowess and discern whatever higher power is at hand. If it's a wild thing like Bez, so be it. Deity is ever near yet rarely in full view. Nor may you know its name.

Bulfinch's fine baby boy endures this universal crisis of birth superbly, faring far better in the process than his fainthearted father. He grows by the usual fits and starts, eventually to manhood. So does his father grow to manhood, as a baby brother appears in years to come. And this makes them all proud of themselves, and of each other. And then at last a baby girl arrives, with two sturdy big brothers to help Bez tend her.

Bulfinch, each time exuberant with new-dad ecstasy, bounds back to his desk and career, struggles, straggles, retreats, advances – all the usual career crap. Now he's retired, reposing in the sun, watching grandchildren do crazy dances, like Bez. But with a lawn sprinkler. Grandpa will soon get hosed, of course. So this is a narrative wanting in wisdom. Bez, watching from somewhere, somehow sees the wisdom in that.

Rajeshwar Prasad, born in Bela, Aurangabad, Bihar, India, on 26 August 1970, is a poet, playwright, novelist, essayist, researcher, philosopher, thinker, and academician. He is a prominent figure in English literature who infuses meaningful philosophical insights into appealing stories. With a Ph.D. exploring Christopher Marlowe's lyricism and many years of service as a Professor, he draws on the strengths of both worlds. He is the author of many thought-provoking plays, including *The Travellers, The Wife, The Tribute, Zero into Four, Teachers' Day,* and *Zero into Nine*; the insightful fiction, "Righteousness"; and collections of powerful poetry, including Gandhi – the Messiah and Bullet Land, all published by TSL Publications, Rickmansworth, UK.

His epic, *The Gandhi-Gita,* the novels Dance of Democracy and *Now, Forever Yours,* and the reflective essays in *Hello Life* show the author's scope. His life of teaching and creative writing demonstrates his commitment to enhancing mind and soul. He has been honoured with several national and international awards in Literature and Education. He has also published 26 research articles, 9 essays, short stories, and poems. His philosophical, humane, and thought-provoking articles were featured in *The Aerial Perspective,* Quillkeepers Press, LLC, US, and were widely admired and read. He was awarded the 'Asian Excellence Award 2024' for the 'Best Professor of the Year', the 'Award of Excellence' for the 'Indian Icon Educational Entrepreneur', 2 Times 'Golden Book Awards' for his books *Zero Into Four* and *Dance of Democracy,* 2 Times 'Sahitya Sparsh Awards' for his books *The Travellers* and *Gandhi – the Messiah* 'Top 10 Rising Leaders Awards', 'Top 100 Leaders Awards' and 'Ukiyoto Literary Awards' for his fiction '*Righteousness*', Visionary Indians Award 2025, and National Teacher of the Year Awards 2025. For him, teaching and writing are not merely professions but sustenance for the soul – endeavours that allow him to continuously engage with and contribute to the literary and philosophical discourse.

A Father's Current

Bela, where black and mixed soils merge, draws its soul from the northward Adari River. A paradox, wide yet dry for much of the year, Adari awakens with fearsome monsoon grace, its deep waters a dance with destiny, miraculously sparing human lives. More than a waterway, it is the village's living heart.

On its western bank, a verdant tapestry of trees frames the landscape, a serene boundary to eastern homes. Under the moon's silver gaze, families gather on rooftops, watching the river reflect the heavens – a poignant communion where the river embraces the moon, leaving humanity to beautiful, solitary existence. From lads swimming for hours to meditating elders, all are drawn to its timeless allure.

On the other side of the river, emerald paddy passes into golden wheat and mustard that take on an endless green. There, among it all, is Bela's oldest peepal tree, a watchful guardian of Goddess Kali's temple, forever shielding her from encroachment. According to myth, Kashi Singh went blind due to disrespect, while the holy tree changed its appearance to reflect Bela's unshaken belief, amazingly still unseen.

Here, one can find life-giving and fatal powers coexisting closely. Through the five crematoria and a graveyard, the place vaguely recalls the lives that arrived and departed, and witnesses the common denominator: an incessant desire. Yet, alongside these, memorials stand sentinel, witnessing life's continuity as families honour the past.

Bela, a village of five thousand souls, boasts eighteen temples echoing devotion. On the Maghra, Saptami, every year, at the Kirtan Sthala, there are 24-hour *"Hare Ram, Hare Krishna"* chants, uniting hearts in profound community. This is Bela: a vibrant tapestry of nature's majesty, human spirit, enduring faith, and life's quiet, beautiful rhythm.

Jagdip, a man famed for his truthfulness, nonviolence, and honesty, lived in the aforementioned tapestry of the Kirtan Sthala, Adari, and the temple of Goddess Kali.

Despite knowing how to sign, which he learned from Dhanu, one of his distant blood relatives and neighbours, he remained illiterate due to the village's lack of education and frequent tragedies.

He was not formally educated, but he had more knowledge and insight than the educated people in his community at the time. He claimed that the essence of every society and religion is "well to all" and possessed a thorough practical understanding of life, death, society, the world, philosophy, and metaphysics.

He was among the admirers of Mahatma Gandhi and the Hindu-Muslim union. He used to claim that his unusually lengthy hands were the sign of his divine nature, having once seen Mahatma Gandhi.

People used to say, "Jagdip was born into a peasant family at the home of his maternal uncle, Bhaju, in the Dadhapi village, Aurangabad, Bihar, India, to his unfortunate mother and father, Deni, who died of smallpox when he was 19 days old. So, he was fostered by his grandparents and the great-grandparents with the help of some relatives and neighbours of his own remote family."

There was a minimal chance of his survival due to his then condition of the widespread, repeated smallpox, plague, and cholera every year. In those days, there were no good medical facilities, and the same happened again. So, dozens of people in the village died of cholera, plague, and smallpox every year. People expected his sudden death and the end of the dynasty with him. Whatever, but Dhanu and Prabhu helped him in childhood and continued to do so throughout his life.

Jagdip was never free of problems, and they surrounded him throughout his life. But he was a man not to look back, and he usually spent his life that way. In his childhood, at about 11, he was married, though he did not live with his wife because she lived with her mother, a custom prevalent in the area at the time: a newly married woman would go to her marital home after at least 1 year. Unfortunately, his wife died during this time in her maternal home.

As a result, Bhagwati from Ratanpura, who hails from a village less than six kilometres away, became

Jagdip's wife. She was a woman from a very prominent family. They have twelve kids during their marriage, but only three are still surviving today, with the other nine having passed away.

In the meantime, Jagdip's second son, Ganesh, died from an electric shock. He was so sad and shocked at the death of his child. He was speechless for some days and totally amazed by what had happened to him.

He was already broken by the death of his second son, and he had also to bear the responsibility to care for Ganesh's young children – Kushum, Reshami, and Bipin – and maintain the joint family. But he survived this terrible tragedy and ran the family so well that all his affairs were handled correctly, allowing him to live a normal life.

It is well accepted that tragedy never occurs alone. Some of the villagers were not in a position to aid him because of jealousy, but they were able to torment him as much as they could, and they did just that. Not a year passed without something being taken from his property, or without tube wells and starters being stolen to harass him.

The potato crop was occasionally stolen, as was the wheat, flaxseed, gram, or paddy crop. Since his entire joint family relied on agriculture, he found it challenging to live in that situation.

Despite three recorded canals in the village, there was not enough water in any of them to irrigate. As a result, he had three tube wells that watered his unirrigated land, which totalled around sixteen acres. This was a cause for envy, and some of the villagers often tried to harm him. Thus, they occasionally stole motors or starters. Consequently, he faced huge monetary setbacks, and his crops were destroyed. But his spiritual condition grew more capable of supporting him and educating his boys, grandkids, and girls.

He would tell his sons and grandkids to pursue their education at all costs, and he would sacrifice his own body for theirs and for the sake of education.

"My dears, continue your education at all costs," he used to tell them.

He frequently said, "A neat and clean society, the advancement of humanity and the globe, and education are the foundations of success. Like Gandhi, be a citizen of the world and spread the message of truth and nonviolence. I will sell my body to educate you for your learning."

There were times in his life when he didn't have the money to cover his children's expenses. However, he was content with the state of scarcity rather than apprehensive. Under these circumstances, he approached some known people for help, and he repaid the dues when the crops were harvested from his fields. When the vegetable crops were harvested, he sold them and honestly paid the grocers. Thus, they were quite pleased with him and commended his honesty and commitment to the Life Force.

They said, "You are a man of extraordinary Life Force, and this is the rare gift to you. You are so sincere and eager to see your loved ones educated, yet you are completely uneducated yourself."

"Your honour," Jagdip answered with a smile.

He said further, "I can tell the difference between good and evil. I have equal faith in God and the material things of this world. I conduct my life by my beliefs."

On occasion, he received the advance to pay for his children's education or to complete other household tasks. However, somebody stole the crops. He had to consider his alternatives to deal with this double sock circumstance.

However, he wasn't frightened in this scenario and handled it with great pleasure. He said that this will provide him with a discovery and the opportunity to learn something new that will benefit his life and experience.

"We should welcome both joys and sorrows equally," he proclaimed.

He said, "Both good and evil reside in this universe, and both forces are constantly at work without cessation. We should not lose our patience; rather, we should see it as an opportunity to live in this strange circumstance."

No matter what he possessed, he was always content. He urged other villagers and family members to treat all circumstances in life equally, whether they be happiness or sadness. No one in the world has ever disregarded the fact that life has two sides, both of which are part of the same existence, according to him. The tests are so difficult that even a saint has to take them. He also stated that misery and grief affect both good and bad people. However, the world values virtues while abusing evils.

"Joys and sorrows are the two sides of the same life, which cannot be separated. So, we all should continue our life's journey, usually," he stated.

He used to tell people, "The elements of grief and misery have created me. My great-grandfather, Akhaj, a 60-year village-headman, and grandfathers Bhola and Jimedari, passed away from smallpox when I was a minor, between 2 pm and 9 pm on the same day. My widowed mother couldn't bear the catastrophe of my father's death. She divorced me and married a man in Tiwari Bigha."

He continued, "I have carried several biers of my family members – from my home to the crematorium – my son Ganesh, my wife Bahgwati, my daughter-in-law, my grand niece, and nine of my kids, are among them. In light of all of this, this is not a decision that would change my life. Life Force, which constantly motivates me to handle everything in a way that benefits humanity and the world."

Even though he was the unfortunate son of unfortunate parents, he was a lucky man for the entire community. He would assist and support the villagers who were in need, especially during their hard times. He was a man who was always there to care for his family and care for the people in his community. He used to give financial assistance without interest if any of them needed assistance while planting or purchasing oxen. He assisted them all and told them to return the dues after the harvest.

The paddy demonstration started in July. Therefore, some villagers didn't have the funds to purchase oxen to cultivate their fields, and folks began preparing between April and June. He approached them in this circumstance without their invitation and offered to help. Some of them went so far as to ask him for financial assistance. Always, he willed to help them. As a result, their lives went on as usual, and they were spared the predicted loss.

Wedding costs were exorbitant in his culture, particularly for a girl's marriage. The dowry system was also common. Some individuals struggle to pay for these costs due to financial difficulties. However, Jagdip was there to assist them during these moments. To cover such costs, he would give them grain or cash without charging any interest. If a daughter's wedding took place.

When a dacoit broke into his wife's maternal home, it was an unforgettable occurrence. Dacoits looted everything from his home. He didn't even have a blanket in the home in Ratanpura. Every piece of the kitchenware was looted. The looting of funds occurred. Their lives were spared, thankfully. People's lives have been rescued. Rameshwar, the son of his brother-in-law, arrived the next morning to tell him about the awful incident.

Rameshwar said, "O, my uncle, fortunately, I was spared, but all utensils, all quilts and blankets, all cash amounts and silver coins, and all other household goods have been stolen. My house doesn't even have a bowl."

"My heart-beat, don't worry," Jagdip said with great philosophical conviction.

He convinced him, saying, "Kings have never been made of robbers and thieves. They are consistently on the same path of wickedness. Their misdeeds are revealed one day – in court as well as by the Lord – and they are punished here and there."

"I am with you," he said further.

Rameshwar said, "But...how?"

Jagdip replied, "There won't be any issues. Let it go. Live a regular life. You will get justice at the time. You will have plenty of property."

After saying this, he organised the necessary quilts, sheets, utensils, and other household items for Rameshwar's home, and then went with him to Ratanpura to help him. To allay his fears of the looters, he spent a few days with him.

He assisted them whenever they needed it, not just sometimes. When one was sick, one would visit them at home every day to inquire about any financial difficulties with therapy or other assistance. He would assist them if that were the case. Additionally, he transported them to the hospital on his shoulders because, in those days, rural areas lacked communication infrastructure, and villagers would carry the sick on their shoulders.

He utilises three tube wells to irrigate his property. Some impoverished individuals lacked tube wells and had less land, leaving them reliant on others with tube wells to cultivate vegetables on their property. In this condition, Jagdip provided irrigation water for their fields.

The most well-known individual in the community was Jagdip, who was adored by members of all thirteen castes and groups. He was their pathfinder, someone who never insulted, mistreated, hurt or threatened anybody. On the other hand, he loved them and assisted them with all of their needs out of pure respect.

One of his relatives from Dihuri, Manoj, has enough respect for him to follow his rules. Manoj considers him to be his teacher and mentor. He accompanied him on every step of his life. He claims that Jagdip's advice to him was more valuable than the world's pearls and diamonds.

"He is the only man whose ideas shed light on us," Manoj said.

Manoj says, "He is the only one who created me and my bright future. Anyone who follows the routes he has established will never experience hardship or failure in life. He is more than pearls and diamonds for me. He is like a lighthouse to me, and he helped me find my bright way, and he is my whole universe."

Jagdip was deeply shocked and lived with an unbroken heart when his gentle and humane friends, Madho, Makun, and Murlidhar, died over the years, and he was left alone. He often remembered them and said philosophically, "Life is a passing dream."

With the money he made from farming, he purchased around five acres of property, and by the time he passed away, he owned all sixteen acres. He died of a brain haemorrhage, untimely and unexpected, a couple of years back on his way to a hospital in Gaya, in his more than 81 years of age. The whole village emerged to pay tribute to such a great spirit and mourned the loss of his life, which was so sad.

In the village, his funeral march was also unusual, with a sizable crowd of people – men, women, children, and adults – weeping for his death, which was never seen. The populace of all castes and communities gave him hundreds of shrouds when he passed away. As a result, his bier grew too heavy for people to carry it from his home to the crematorium on their shoulders. So, some shrouds were thrown straight into the fire during cremation. His body was changed into the five elements at the bank of the Adari River, the place where he spent his whole life.

He is no longer here, but his legacy is even more impressive. He gave up many things so the future would be bright. His children and grandchildren – Ramnaresh, a teacher; Dashrath, a local politician; Rajeshwar, a professor, poet, playwright, novelist, essayist, researcher, philosopher, thinker, and academician; Amod, a teacher; Bipin, a postal employee; Ashutosh, a bank employee; Rajnish, Ujjwal, and Uttam, engineers; Prabhat, an assistant professor; and Manish, Ranju, Sangita, and Amrita, home aides – all are the living embodiments of his principles. His core belief that education is the best tool for humanity and the world is reflected in all his professional endeavours, including teaching and engineering. Their victory is evidence of their continuing legacy and lives on as his living legacy.

His commemorative, placed next to the Adari River and close to the river bridge, is the sentinel of the whole village, and the people say his spirit is still there, leading and caring for them. On the occasion of his death anniversary, they gather there, pay homage, and offer his image with luminous and vibrant flowers.

His ashes were immersed by his distant cousin Ramlakhan and his son Ramnaresh in the holy *Ganges* in Varanasi, which flows into the Indian Ocean through it and into the Bay of Bengal, spreading the flame of virtues and natural wisdom like the natural plants to all mankind and the world.

Each day, Pradip, a distant cousin, will clean and maintain the memorial carefully to keep it proper and in good condition. People go there, and pay homage by saying, "Here, a spirit lies, whose name is written in water – who lived for us; who untimely and abruptly left us; but leaving a rich legacy of truth, nonviolence, honesty, fraternity, justice, equality, and dedication to education. One who raised us, impacted us too much, showed us the path of virtues, and mentored us! We salute such a magnificent spirit!"

Reema M Raj is an engineer by profession and a writer by heart. She is currently based out of Mumbai but consider herself to be a world citizen. Travelling feeds her soul, and they are passionate about sharing their journey through words.

I like me better when ...

Dear Aadi,

People say it is difficult to make new friends in your thirties. We are set in our ways, are cautious about new people, and don't easily let them in. I also believed it to be true, of course. That was before I met you.

After working from home due to COVID policy, we were all asked to return to the office. I barely knew anyone at work because I was new to the organization, and my current team wasn't working at the same location. Since my divorce, I retreated into my shell, as I didn't feel like my usual extroverted self. I lacked the energy to make the effort to interact with new people around me. I just knew two people: a friend from a previous organization and a recently introduced colleague. This was my routine: I would work all day and only socialize with those two individuals at lunch. I have always been part of a bigger social circle at work, so this situation felt different.

My separation was a difficult time for me. I fell back on my girlfriends for emotional support. I was in survival mode, and they checked up on me to make sure I was okay. I somehow lost touch with all my guy friends. I felt a lot of hurt and betrayal in my marriage, and I believe that after that, I unconsciously kept men out. Even at work, my teammates and managers were ALL WOMEN. And then out of nowhere, you popped up.

I still remember the first time I saw you. You were wearing your Brooklyn 99 tee and your striking grey hair and beard, which you carried with an air of confidence. We made eye contact as we passed each other and smiled politely.

A mutual friend introduced us a few days later, and we began spending time together at work. The first thing I noticed about you was the kindness in your eyes. You were chivalrous, polite, and seemed fun. It was easy being around you. Our mutual love of working out, food, travel, and adventure was something that brought us together.

We attended 'Devils Circuit,' an obstacle competition, and it cemented our friendship. You motivated and supported me through all their challenges. Being an adventure junkie, I felt like myself again after a really long time. Our conversations usually revolve a lot around pushing each other to be better. You have inspired me to run regularly, and hopefully, I have done the same for you with respect to strength training. I have been listening to you talk about joining a gym for a year now. Hopefully, that happens soon. If not, you lose the bet, and I win a lot of money.

We have all these things in common, but we also stand at opposite sides of the spectrum in many areas. I am talkative, and you are a man of few words. I speak my heart out, and you like to keep your cards close to your chest. I am an emotional decision-maker, and you are a logical one. I love pulling your leg, and you love it too. You often act serious, which makes it heartwarming for me to annoy you.

We drove to another city for that competition, and for the first time, you were in a shared space. You were so relaxed while driving and opened up to me like never before. I saw a deeply sensitive side to you. Your car broke down, and we ended up spending a couple of hours at the side of the highway. We were in our private bubble that evening.

We have been best friends for a year now, and you have been my rock. You are the first person I think of when something good or bad happens to me. I think of myself as tough and someone who can keep her emotions in check. When I discuss something upsetting with my girlfriends, I tend not to cry. But when I talk to you about the same things, the opposite happens. My walls collapse, my nervous system relaxes, and my floodgates open. *I have the luxury to be vulnerable with you.* You are my perfect listener, and it helps me calm down. This year, you have seen me go through multiple highs and lows. I am working through all of it in therapy—phases of loneliness, anxiety, and panic attacks—and you have stood by me through it all. Sometimes I picked fights with you for no fault of your own, but you didn't run away or let me go. You held on even though I am a mess.

The only thing that annoys me about you is that you don't open up to me. You never vent to me when something is bothering you. I have to pull it out of you, and even then, I only receive a sentence or two at most. Would it kill you to let me help you every once in a while? To let me be there for you like you are for me? I can see you love protecting, taking care of, and being there for me by any means necessary. I would love to be there for you as well if you just let me.

I had a powerful force field around me that repelled men. Upon reflection, I realized I had been surrounded by only women for a couple of years. And you somehow broke through all my barriers and continue to be my friend. The center diamond of my crowning jewel. I love you, and I am grateful that you are part of my life!

You are my cheerleader, and you uplift me. You are thrilled to see me succeed. I want to see myself through your lens. You have taught me to rely on and focus on myself. Your friendship is a comforting blanket, and your smile lights up my world, and I truly hope we remain besties for life.

I like me better when I am with you.

Love,

Riii

Rathin Bhattacharjee from Kolkata, India,
graduated from Calcutta University. He joined
Bhutan Civil Service Commission as an English
Teacher in 1990. Awarded His Majesty's Gold Medal
(2018) for Lifetime Achievement in Teaching, he has
been published and anthologised extensively. His
novel, *The Damon in Doctor's Disguise* on Web
Novel has won critical acclaim. His latest book *'I
Love You' in the ICU & 20 Other Stories* has been
nominated for The Legacy of The Literature Prize,
2025. He loves writing, blogging, translating,
critiquing, and editing.

Barda, Debesh Bhattacharya : The Man with the Never-Say-Die-Attitude.

The other day, while trying to write about *Bardi*, Mrs. Tapati Bhatta, I had what in literary parlance is generally called the writer's block. I was lost, not knowing what to write about and how to go about it. I had serious doubts about whether I was qualified enough to write about these people others hold close to their hearts, and that gave me the idea of writing about them in the first place. In a few words, I had serious doubts about my own abilities and the very purpose of my trying to write about people long gone! Something at the back of my mind, though, was urging me all the while not to give up. I haven't yet, and you readers will wake up to the reality of letting me know, in due course, if my efforts have been worthwhile.

Today I find myself in a thick soup once again, my mind clouded once more, unsure how much I really know about my Barda, Debesh Bhattacharya, and also because of my great fondness for him. I wrote a couple of years back to my Australian sis-in-law, Dr. Ellen McEwen:" I love Barda a lot because I can see beneath the rough and harsh exterior, a very good human being..." and it was no exaggeration.

Debesh Bhattacharya was born on 15th March 1941. The eldest son of Jogesh Bhattacharyya, he was fearless and often found himself against heavy odds. He was once said to have been awakened in the middle of his sound sleep by his furious father and beaten black and blue for apparently no fault of his. But his determination, coupled with his strong willpower, had seen him through the worst of times and stood him in good stead. When preparing for the I.A., he realized his weakness in Maths just after the trial, deported himself to his maternal grandpa's house in Bhawanipore and under the able tutelage of *Mejomama* (maternal uncle), who was a maths wizard of some sort, sharpened his wits so far as the troublesome subject was concerned. He secured letter marks (above 80%) in Maths in the Board Exam. He went on to the prestigious Presidency College, Calcutta, to study for an Honours degree in Economics and subsequently completed his Master's degree from the University of Calcutta. He was justifiably proud that he did not stay *bekar*, unemployed, for a single day in his entire life! He was offered a job before the M.A. result was out.

Having realized the financial doldrums his family was in, he left for foreign shores. He must have been driven by his insatiable hunger to excel at the highest level, and his love for his motherland just added fuel to the fire. In his sojourn for newer pastures, he did very well in the U.K., the U.S.A., New Zealand, and Australia. But what finally drew him to the last named country to settle down there was Australia's neutral attitude to racism in those days, and my sis-in-law, Dr. Ellen McEwen. I heard him talking matter-of-factly so often about what had ended his prolonged bachelorhood, with *Baud*i going back to Melbourne in a huff and puff and *Barda* coming to terms with the first pangs of true love, that it was like watching a Broadway Classic over and over again. Baudi turned out to be the best thing in his life, and they stayed inseparable for god knows how long.

Despite his differences with *Baba* over every subject under the sun, well, almost, my late father was genuinely fond of *Barda*. Ma was no less, if not more. And both of them had reasons to be. Barda might have taken some time to establish himself in the foreign land, but once he found a firm foothold, there was no stopping him from discharging his filial and brotherly duties. He assured the relatives time and again that they would not be burdened with any member of our late father, Jogesh Bhattacharyya's family, and do not you forget, dear reader, it was quite large, if *Baba* could not recover from the aftermath of his 17-year-long case against the state government, which he went on to win.

If all the children of Lt.J.C. Bhattacharyya are well-settled today and have done creditably for themselves, then, besides the grace of The Almighty, it is due to the belief each one of them has had deep down over the years, that Barda would always be there for them. Along with *Mejdi*, Mrs. Arati Guha, *Barda* had always kept the family flag flying. His contributions to the family are so many that they are beyond the scope of anything of the size and stature of this article. I personally feel that Lt.J.C. Bhattacharyya's family is privileged to have such a distinguished and disinterested self-seeker. His greatness lies in his love for the family, which has not been confined to immediate family members but has extended to anyone very remotely related to the family.

Let me narrate an incident in this context. Despite owning 3 houses in Sydney, Australia, by dint of his merit and hard work, I never saw Barda wearing a ring on any of his fingers. I learned why he detested having to wear any rings from what he told my spouse once. When our late father's family was going through some rough financial times, one day our Ma asked Barda to pawn one of her gold rings at a local shop. Barda did as he was bid, but he must have been extremely humiliated by having to borrow money from a shopkeeper by pawning his mother's ring! No wonder he never wore a ring!

Even at 72, the hunk of a man that *Barda* was, he was fond of biryani, chicken kabab, and rasgollas, and, despite the doctor's warning, did not let go of any opportunity of devouring them, whenever *Baud*i was not around. He was a fantastic ambassador of India and his life, a glimmer of hope for any young Indian trying to make it big anywhere in the world.

I cannot prove the authenticity of my claim, and no offence is meant to the great Indian batter, Sachin Tendulkar. Still, I am very sure that *Barda* retired early (he could have continued till quite late in his life as an Associate Professor of Economics at the University of Sydney, to spend his last years watching the exploits and heroics of the master-blaster!). He could never tire of watching the maestro bat and having his fill. I guess, in some ways, *Barda* identified himself with Sachin, with the pent up fury and frustration of the Indians being treated as second-class citizens, even post-independence, every time he found the master-class belting the opponents, the only way he could.

And this was what had me worried lately. It might have been a matter of coincidence, but he fell seriously ill on his return to Australia from India a few days after Sachin's retirement was officially announced. With Sachin hanging up his bat, Life was bound to lose much of its frolic and fun. The only comfort was knowing that he was in safer hands with his beloved wife of over 35 years and that both his daughters were happily married; things were bound to brighten and turn for the better.

Let me wind up my tribute to Barda with one of the best lessons I learned from him. We were staying at "Nilanjana", the third-floor apartment that he had bought from a famous Bengali actor. He was packing up to go back to Australia. I was a college student then, and for some reason, I wanted his shiny black shoes. After a lot of thought, I could not resist the temptation of blandly asking for the pair. The look of — how do I describe it? The abhorrence that I noticed in his eyes was something that taught me never to beg anything, even from the closest of relatives, for the rest of my life. It was not that Barda was tight-fisted or anything like that; he had given away a lot of things to a lot of people, but he wanted his youngest brother to learn the values of diligence and self-respect. And that incident sums up my late eldest brother in my eyes, in the final analysis.

Jesmal Jalal comes from Kerala, India. He published his debut novel, *The Devil's Cage*, in 2019. His works appeared in *Wild Greens* (USA), *The Galpa* (India), *LIGHT*(USA), and several publications.

The Unwanted Book

I looked at that book on my shelf. Even though I didn't like it, I admired the book very much. It's strange, isn't it? I think so too. It's a souvenir of an act my dad did—

 an ordinary act to anyone who had seen it, but in reality, there lies a great lesson he had taught me. It takes me back to that day in Trivandrum city.

It was a sweltering evening in Trivandrum city. My father and I occasionally visited the city in a year, about once a month. There was always something new to watch every time we came to the city. Sometimes it's a unique fair; sometimes it's a special exhibition. Not to mention the arrival of new guests in the city zoo. And also the various competitions arranged at Gandhi Park. The city never lacked ideas to entertain us.

This time, we were headed to a fair at Kanakakkunnu Palace. The fair was held on the sprawling grounds in front of the prestigious palace. It's a major activity hub in the city. Each time a fair is announced, it has a specific theme. I think the theme that day was 'The roots of Kerala.' I remember seeing so many traditional and cultural displays that day.

It's funny how I got my ticket to enter. My father tricked the cashier into giving me a low-cost ticket for kids under 6. I was seven. The cashier just peeked at me through the small hole used to receive cash. No one could tell the difference.

We entered the fest through a majestic arch placed at the gate. It was elegantly decorated with cutouts of various art forms of Kerala. Kathakali and Mohiniyattam took the main attraction at the centre.

I glanced across the various tables arranged in a row on both sides as we strolled. Clay sculptures, glowing, lively paintings, old hats and umbrellas woven from coconut leaves—everything produced a nostalgic beauty. It was a long but exciting walk.

Although, to be honest, I wasn't interested in those displays. Even though the fest was based on a theme, it had small stalls with toys and video games like a regular fair. So naturally, my eyes went to those instead.

My father is a peculiar man. I had never seen him waste a single penny. So, despite my brutal struggles, he didn't buy me any video games from the stalls. Instead, he bought me cake and sugarcane juice from the kitchen stall located adjacent to those video game stalls. I looked hungrily at those video games while sipping the juice. That's all I could do.

My father's second-most-frequent and well-known phrase was 'Don't waste a single dime on anything we don't truly need.' His first was 'Go and study! Or else no television for a week.'

We were nearing the exit of the fest. Near the exit, there were so many Malayalam books for sale. I loved books, especially Malayalam storybooks. When it came to buying books, my father showed no miserliness. He wanted me to read as many books as he could. Because he himself had a time when he wanted to read but had little money to buy books. Behind his sweet smile lies a past of misery and hard work amidst poverty. He collected used books and studied them hard, which resulted in earning a good job under the state government. Reading saved him from misery.

He bought me the storybooks I wanted. He also bought a book for himself. The book was based on money management. *Not surprising at all!*

Just then, my dad approached a pale old man who was sitting at a lonely corner. He had a small table in front of him with two bundles of books. Interestingly, both bundles contained the same book. My father smiled at the old man and bought a book. I was told to hold it. It had a cheap book cover and looked more like a magazine than a book.

As we walked out of the exit, I ran my eyes over the book. It was a Malayalam poetry book. I was surprised.

"It's a poetry book!" I exclaimed.

"Yes," replied he, coldly.

"Dad, you don't like poetry books," I remarked in wonder.

"No, I don't. But you might like it." He proceeded to walk again.

"Dad, you know that I don't like poetry either."

He let out a sigh. "Whatever! You just keep it."

Whatever? I couldn't understand him. *Why is he acting so differently now?*

"You always tell me not to waste money on anything we don't need," I said with aspiration. "Then why did you buy this book? It's of no use."

He turned back and took that book from me. Then he leaned down and showed me the back cover. The author's photo was displayed on the cover. I recognized him instantly.

"That old man," I muttered.

"Yes, my boy." He said as he patted my head. "He was selling his own book in this age. His bundles were untouched until we approached him. And that's the only book he had. He needed money. He needed appreciation. I just wanted to help him."

"But—"

"Sometimes we do things that give us no gain but help other people." His words reverberated in my ears. "It's humanity. It's just what *we* are."

I couldn't grasp that statement clearly at that moment. I simply thought he was just giving away his money to help the old man—an act out of sympathy. But later, I realized what he did. It was not an act of kindness. It was a token of appreciation for his book. I hadn't cared to look at that old man's face after we bought his book. Since I am a writer now, I could now see what his face reflected. I know what it feels like. That happiness when someone buys your book. That feeling when you know that someone is putting off their precious time to read your book. My dad is a remarkable person. He did what little he could do to make this world a better place. He didn't consider it a great deal. He thought of it as a fundamental quality of being humane.

Once again, I stared at that book to digest that experience in Trivandrum. Just to remind me that sometimes you do gainless things because it's the right thing to do. It's just what we are.

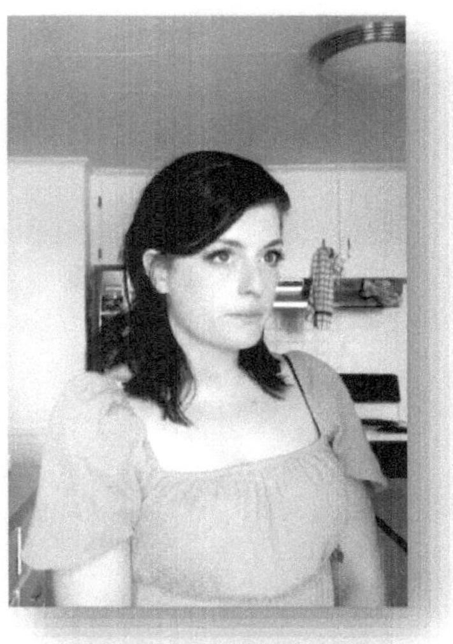

Amanda Izzo is a writer and mixed-media artist from Boston, MA. After years of writing privately, she's begun to share detailed recollections of her life and youth in the form of creative nonfiction. In the hopes of connecting with other readers and shy creatives alike. Recently, her work has been published in *Levitate Magazine, Braver Collective,* and *Oddball Magazine.*

Tell Me Where It Hurts

The first truly cohesive memory I have starts with me falling. It's almost as if my avatar flipped on mid descent as I barreled towards the bottom of a pitch dark boat. I can't recall what I was doing beforehand; if I had tripped on the rug, if a wave took me over, or if I simply didn't look down to see the open floor hatch. I just remember the fall. It felt as if it lasted an eternity while splintering, burning pain seared up the side of my body, ankle to shoulder.

Hitting the wooden floor beneath with a loud thud, a child's scream echoed through the mechanics cabin before it occurred to me that it was my own. The only light came from the hatchway cut out far above me. Just then, two arms sank down to meet me halfway. I stood quickly as they grabbed my underarms and hauled me up effortlessly in one swoop.

"It's ok, you're ok. Tell me where it hurts," my dad lay me across his lap, holding my head against his chest, while he rocked my upper body. No intelligible sounds escaped my mouth, only hyperventilating whimpers and whines.

"Hey, you're ok! I've got you," he rubbed my arm, and a shriek broke the unremitting cadence of my sobbing. My dad's muscles tensed as he flinched from the shock of my pained cry. He loosened his grip around me, extending his neck backwards to get a closer look at me. Feeling his chest drift away, I slunk back into him, closing the gap between us so I could rise and fall in time with his breaths, which were becoming more uncontrolled and rapid.

"It's alright, you're alright. Tell me where it hurts, Panda," his calm reassurance slowly chipped away as he began inspecting my limbs for visible signs of injury. Whether it was a symptom of shock or trying to identify all of the areas of pain that overwhelmed me, I was rendered speechless.

"Tell me...," he was going to repeat himself, but he trailed off, seeing my yellowing skin shift shades of mauve and blue down my thigh and arm that was pressed against him. Splinters of all shapes and sizes stung me from scraping my entire side down the roughly cut wood as I fell. His grip gently tightened around me, as he let out a big sigh and laid his head atop mine.

"...you're alright."

Feeling his guilt and desperation for my own relief, I found the strength to mutter words of reassurance in return.

"I...I...I'm...all...alright."

He kissed the top of my head and began slowly rocking me, in time with but opposite the waves.

"Yeah, you are."

A.J.R. Mennon is an author from India.

A Father's Monday.

DAWN

Will you wake up today? Isn't it time to brush your teeth, bathe, light the incense, and make the tea? Wear a good shirt today with the maroon necktie. Yes, it's turned reddish-brown of late, but it should do. It's the only good one you've got, and it's got to be a little tighter today. "You need to sweat", as the new GM snarled yesterday.

Last night's smoke and drink coil around your head with their weight, but you'd better resist their conclusion till the day's end. Peak mornings are turning heavier and darker, but come on. Move those flaccid limbs. Let your sole feel the frigid tile. What's the date? It's the eighteenth of April. Toss and turn and twitch all you want— the bulk of this heaviness is here to stay.

Wash the blood away. It's time for a new razor. This one's blunted and rusted. And again, you applied too much pressure. Your bald spot seems to have grown an inch or two. Your eyes are drooping, and your face is all puffed up. But it cannot matter at this hour. Thirty-five thousand to the EMI for the flat back home. Twenty-five for their rent in the city. Fifteen for their car's EMI. Twenty thousand more for his school's fee. And twenty for her monthly expenses…and the rest to squeeze out the debts and survival here. Take care not to slip into dreams of a simpler life you'd enjoy without these. Too early for that. Just tie your tie— the hour's dying away. Make sure to fasten it neatly and check thrice before leaving the house; Payday's two weeks away.

Perhaps you should have eaten something. Just black tea on an empty stomach for another long day may not suffice. Well, either way is the same: It's going to hit fifty degrees outside. No amount of food is enough to help one endure that without bleeding his energies. The traffic is not going to help today either— of all days. Don't forget that you need to visit the head-office-shrine to pick up those three pending contracts before returning to the field to finalize all three. There will be hell to pay if we don't meet yet another month's target. Don't use the elevator today. It might be better for you to start taking the stairs. Only five flights. That, too, downward into the basement car park.

Yet you're heaving and sweating, and your shirt feels a little wet on the back. Of course, now you regret not picking up the fitness program the building committee drew up for the residents. You could've shed this belly and maybe even put on some muscle to have the energy for these important days. Regret is another waste of energy in the morning. You can go to the gym by yourself this weekend to try to start again. The lady from Eighteen-D might be there like that one day. Maybe you can talk to her instead of just awkwardly returning her smile. She seemed a bit too keen to take an interest in your life— that's the issue. It's like she's trying to draw water from an old well that dried up too long ago. It gets rather annoying. She's still a sweet person, though. Wonder what she does for a living.

Anyhow. It's eight already. You were right to skip breakfast. Have a heavy lunch instead. Rush to the car, fire up the engine, and leave the AC on for a few minutes to cool things inside. Need to touch the road before the sun climbs further over our heads. Don't forget to give Usman money for cleaning the car. He's planning on visiting his wife back home next month. His smile—which was brighter than a noon sun—struck with a peculiar sharpness when talking about her last night. He's a good kid. Only needs to learn how to clean the car better. There are dust marks over the wheel arches. Well, he's young enough. He will learn. Cleaning cars all day in basements for change you'd basically throw away, and he still wears that smile. Twenty years ago...when you landed out here, did you once wear a smile like that?

NOON

"Yes, you left your old company on paper only eight months ago! But you look like you're still rotting there with the way you approach these targets. You expect those contracts to grow legs and sign themselves? And the targets to be met during peak season by crawling at the pace you do? Do you know what it means to be working for this company?! I think you weren't ready for this sort of a jump; Rotting in that same place for the last twelve years...pathetic how lax it makes you!"

Her words barked out —though somewhat understandable— ring persistently in the ears, creating a dull, radiating pain like a tapeworm lodged somewhere behind your head. Yes, you're used to it around this time of the season when the targets and directors are breathing down your neck. But today it made you feel small. Like you yourself were a worm. Now wonder why. At least she didn't say those words in front of the others.

The steering wheel's growing hot under the ruthless sun. As expected, the traffic is doing you no favors by staying frozen. When can you hope to reach the third store and finalize the last contract with that slippery key account's manager from KCM? Having failed to get him to stick thrice, perhaps a fourth time is the charm. The sweat fights the car's AC to glisten up your forehead. Just drink some water and breathe. Like the doctor said last week. Focus on the brown mountain-faces lining the highway where the sunbeams trickle down to carpet the road.

To think, just two more months…two more months and you'd be standing at the Arrivals to see his innocent smile, to hear his excited voice. Remember how, when he was little, he would run up to you laughing and jump up on you? Do you remember the scent of his hair when he hugged you and wouldn't let go? He's a little old for that now. But his eyes and that laugh remain as pure as those times. You can't wait to see his reaction to the new flat you've rented for us, can you? The rent's almost twice as high from the last one, but the boy's never had a room to himself. Nor even an AC. Perhaps, for a month at least, you can facilitate his bliss—and maybe even share in it. Although she's going to be there too. Even if you haven't spoken to her since the day you caught those messages on her phone from the 'friend'. Wonder if they still meet up when he's at school... Ah! You should've just played some damn music. Here come the horns. The traffic's crawling. Better floor it and reach the store. Maybe you can buy that new World Cup-themed football for him. It's only two months from now. They should be in.

The sun is burning your fingers through the windshield. A newer car's AC would've been able to counter it better at this hour. You need to get indoors. Don't forget lunch again. You're on antibiotics, remember? Lunch at Shankaran's mess should do. You've been craving their fried Kingfish with Sambhar rice anyway. Hard to believe they charge so little for the entire meal. Then again, they're mostly frequented by those construction workers. God knows how those souls survive month after month. Looking at them when you eat makes it harder to swallow each one of your morsels— even if they work to fill their own stomachs and pockets. Occasionally, you nurse the notion that this comfortable world would simply collapse if these men chose to step aside one day. At least you have a car and the blessing of the AC for most of the day. One wonders if those guys have children? However, do *they* manage? Take a deep breath now. The light's green.

DUSK

You shouldn't have skipped lunch. At least, traffic flows at a deliberate, leisurely pace now. These cars glide along the highway without jerking stops as if part of a continuum. From how it punished not a handful of hours ago, the sun shows its capacity for clemency by letting up at this hour. What it throws at you right now from behind the clouds is more akin to material made for admiration with a glass of single malt, lazing away on an easy chair, lost in the labyrinth of your warmest memories. Perhaps with the soundtrack from Roja by A.R. R., like you and her once listened to it on one of your sunset drives into the mountains. This country's a sublime sanctuary this time of day, considering how the air sheds all heat as the evening wears on, inviting and making room for the cool desert breeze to graze your skin. If later one had the time, he could relish a barefoot walk along the beach. Maybe treat himself to a fresh shawarma. Never mind, however. You're not tasting such luxury anytime soon. Not until you meet the target, at least.

You should still eat something. Go to the Indian teashop and have a cup with pakoras, or you'll only grow weary and miss the part of the day which makes everything else tolerable. You won't enjoy it on an empty stomach, and you need to arrive before the place is swarmed by annoyingly jolly people. Loosen the grip on the steering wheel a little; it's all getting too sweaty. It's too much pressure.

You're aboard that one train again. But it's still too soon to wonder what kind of family man you've been. Whether you're even a successful one, as she put it last week. Is that why she did it? Hard to pinpoint where it went off the rails over the past 15 years. When and where 'Sneham' died. Does it drop dead at once, or does it bleed out? "Your manhood is fragile, and I'm entitled to my choices!" That's the new favorite phrase. Seems like a promotion. Well, nobody taught you to how to be this man. Who are you to have a say in her freedoms?

Especially when you sit fifteen hundred kilometers away? Her sisters, her friends, surely know better. Perhaps they can make next month's payments? She has the right to choose her freedoms. What rights do you have? But better to not call the advocate again. He's annoyed by your indecision. What's the point of walking away now, after all these years? Who'll pay for both lawyers? Who'll pay the mountain of liabilities the judge is sure to order? And what will happen to him? What if you're kept from seeing the boy anymore? Forget it. You have no power. Just rush to the bar, will you?

"Vasu bhai isn't coming today?" "Annual leave."

"I see. Not loosening the tie today as well, eh."

"One more, straight-up, please. And please keep a new single malt separate…for Home Remedy."

"The one from last week running dry already?"

"Sales target still pending this month and have to pay respects to the money exchange tomorrow."

"Oof. Maybe I should've given you two."

Barman's chuckle seemed sincere. His hairline suggests a moderately long marriage as well—or so a cynic could imagine. You're getting there... fantasizing about the what-ifs ever more often than before. If you weren't losing your hair or could lose this belly, perhaps you could have had something on the side as well with that Filipina sales associate who keeps bringing you the cigarettes with widened eyes. She looks like she'd be in her late twenties. Hopefully, she wouldn't think you're a creep if the next time you see her, you'll take off the ring. Only, the last few times when you've considered doing it, the boy's face appears.

Maybe you should visit the church this weekend. It might be a better remedy. You haven't done so since you saw his eyes meet yours as they brimmed, your hands joined in front of the God who marooned you. The shame may subside if you sit there quietly for a couple of hours. Even if faith has turned faded of late. What do you have to lose? Except sleep.

MIDNIGHT

What do you seek when you stand before the bathroom mirror to stare at yourself like this? What do you wish to feel with every neat sip of that single malt, every drag of that Marlboro? Are you trying to break free from something, or are you curious about why this hazy reflection has grown increasingly transparent over the past six months?

Vasu was talking about quitting and starting up a distribution business back home. You don't doubt his capability or intelligence. Only his discipline. Yes, he's got some good land back home that'll give him a good nest egg to begin with. Still, it's not easy at our age to quit everything like that and start fresh without it burning you in some way. Besides, the way the drink's got a hold on him, one wonders if he even has the health for it. He sleeps and watches TV when not at work. Well, whatever he does, you can only ask him to be cautious. His wife and kid bravely left everything back home to join him here— all to support him. He doesn't want to take that for granted, even if his wife makes more than he does now.

Whatever he may do, let's not pretend you've not had similar thoughts. But what's holding you back

from starting up on your own goes deeper than the
need for deep pockets. It's support. Forget a person's
support, you don't even have any land to call yours
anymore since the last fifteen years. Only the one
flat owned by the bank— for now.

You're too tired anyway...come on, now dive
into another sip. Forget those unrealistic business
ideas, will you? It's not a business that you really
crave, but freedom from the well you've descended
into these past years. The older a man gets, the
harder it is to reverse certain choices. Some are just
impossible. Should a grown man even set much store
by such dreams destined to burn? The spouse labelled
yours as bizarre escapism. They are indeed bizarre.
You've had one of the other kind. A self-similar
dream more than twice over the last six months. One
you've yet to grasp:

It's a slow, sunny afternoon. You're standing
alone in a rice field. It's utterly barren—as in, picked
clean. From the horizon in each direction, colossal
herds of wild zebras are all charging towards you like
a tsunami wave. Or a legion of soldiers. You're gripped
by an excitement and a terror at the same time, unsure
of whether to run or to stand your ground and see if

they crush you or carry you away somewhere. It feels as though you stand on the brink of being awoken. The terror is understandable, but why the excitement? Yes, they were your favorite animal when you were a boy, but why the excitement?

Your chest is tightening. Drink water. Or pour some into the peg and make it lighter. It would be great to not wake up tomorrow, but two more months until you get to see his innocent smile emerging from the crowd, until this room's filled with his laughter late into the night when you play-fight. How will he react to his gift? You can only hope he likes it. His friends all get branded presents from their parents regularly, but you know, despite his age, he understands that you do your best. Never shows ingratitude, even if his little heart wants what his friends have. You've seen it in his eyes, especially when he tries to hide it. A kid with a mature heart. It's a good thing. He's not nearly as demanding as the other kids you've seen around here. God, they're hell.

Anyhow. Knowing that he is respectful and sincere and that he may grow up to be like that does bring you some reprieve, right? Hopefully, the sacrifices will be worth it someday. When everything else in his life seems like a failure, a father's only and most important success can sometimes be his son. If on your deathbed you could see that he makes a respectable man of himself, you could give in to death with a contented smile. A smile as pure as his when he was little. Last year, when he asked you why we didn't stay together, it corroded your heart a little. Maybe he even resents you a little bit for it. And when he's a teenager, he will hate you. You must endure…or you could wear that cold blanket of indifference that many fathers take comfort in. Only…what Vasu confessed to you that day stuck with you. He said his biggest fear was looking into the eyes of a man who used to be his little boy and realizing that, in two blinks, that little boy had vanished forever. And that day, he'd understand what true loss is.

No. You cannot quit this place and go home, despite the times you've even bought tickets and still didn't get on the plane. Only for him. She will be fine, but he won't be. You don't believe that he still sometimes looks at you with admiration, even if those moments are growing further apart as he grows older. It reminds you of something your own father once told you. "A father's sacrifice has only one destiny: Misunderstanding—until you truly grow up."

Well, you don't care if everyone else in the world misunderstands. But you do if he will. Will he ever understand the burden? Will he want to? One day, perhaps, he will even feel what his father's love was. Long after you're gone…it may echo from his chest like the hums of a ghost trapped behind a mirror.

By the by, you forgot to take off your tie. Again. That's the third time in the last five days. It's okay, you're too faded now. Just loosen it a bit and fall into sleep. Remember to wear a fresh one tomorrow, okay? Perhaps the bright red one. It's strange. You only own red ties— only in different shades of red.

DAWN. TUESDAY.

Will you wake up today?

Kenneth M. Kapp lives with his wife in Milwaukee, Wisconsin, writing late at night in his man-cave. He enjoys chamber music and mysteries. Please visit www.kmkbooks.com. He has been nominated for the Pushcart Price. His stories have appeared in more than ninety publications worldwide including the *Saturday Evening Post, October Hill Magazine, EgoPHobia* in Romania, *Lothlorien Poetry Journal* in Ireland, and *The Wise Owl* in India.

Old Josef's Yankle

Rabbi Kahn sat in the synagogue's office worrying on his beard. Old Josef's Yankle was coming to see him in thirty minutes. Mr. Levy, who served as the congregation's president since Adam *haRishon*, the first Adam himself, had taken him aside at the Kiddish after services last Shabbos. *I knew something was afoot when he continued to ask after my family, even tried to ask about my grandchildren yet to be born.*

Mr. Levy, rolling his eyes to heaven, finally said. "It's like this, Rabbi. Old Josef's Yankle wants to speak with you. I know he doesn't come often. Maybe not even since you started serving as rabbi here." *Nu, he needs to remind me I* have served *here; well, for more than thirty years I have served here! My mother of blessed memory was right – what kind of job is a rabbi for a Jewish boy!* "Josef, you may have heard from your predecessor, was a survivor, so we cut him some slack. A couple of times in the '50s, he came and paraded outside the schul on Yom Kippur with a sign: "There is no God." Once on Purim, he came into the sanctuary when the Megillah was being read and shouted that we should tell God to come play dreidel with him. 'He spun Gimel with me in 1940. Took everything. So now it's my turn to spin.' I heard from my own father how hard the war was on Josef. He lost his whole family."

So now his son comes to me. Yankle must be 70, 75. Sitting back in his office chair, the Rabbi slowly turned around, his eyes searching the shelves sagging with the "Big Books" from Talmud to *Seforim* (Religious Tomes). Two shelves in one corner were filled with books on the Kabala. *Not one helps explain the Holocaust. Wer weiss? Who knows? So now Yankle comes to me. Fur was? What for? Tzuris – more worries.*

The Rabbi, completing his turn, placed his hands, palms down, on his desk – *so you'd think Mr. President would tell me if Yankle drinks tea or coffee, likes kichel or donuts. I should have something. He's coming at one, too early for schnaps* – and muttered, "I'll find out soon enough."

~ * ~

Shuffle – thump, shuffle – thump. A knock with an old cane on the doorpost opposite the mezuzah quickly brought Rabbi Kahn back from his meditation. He always focused on the same question before closing his eyes and, time after time, when he'd open them, he'd hear an echo between his ears: "Go on. You're a big boy now. It's all in the Torah. You just have to dig, sometimes not even so deep."

The rabbi pushed himself back from his desk and, waving Yankle to one of the armchairs waiting around a small coffee table, sat down opposite him. "Nu, perhaps I can offer you something to drink or nibble." *Yankle, he must be Yankle. I can see the pain in his eyes.* "You shouldn't worry, I gave up eating meat for Lent." *Lent? I'm not sure when that is. Hopefully, he doesn't either.*

Yankle leaned forward on his cane. "So, I shouldn't worry? Lent is over on Maundy Thursday; this year it was April 25th, in the middle of Passover." He pushed himself back in the seat. "No, I didn't come to eat or drink. But from my father, Old Josef, I have something to give you."

"I'm sorry, I never met your father. I've heard about him, of course. He had a tough life." Rabbi Kahn paused. What more could he say? *I'm fortunate, born in 1955, the year the Dodgers won the Series.* He looked at Yankle, studied his lined face and sunken lips, and wondered if he ever smiled even as a little boy.

Years ago, Mr. Levy had given him a thumbnail sketch of the family's history. "Old Josef, he must have been born old, escaped the camps in 1943. No one ever learned how he survived until liberation. 'I walked,' was all he ever said. His wife was also a survivor – she from Auschwitz. They met in a DP camp after the war; married in 1947. Yankle was born in 1949. They came to the U.S. in 1950, directly to Brooklyn. More than 60 years ago, when our schul hosted an occasional *Melava Malka* meal Saturday night, Yosef came with Yankle. Congregants fussed over the little boy, he couldn't have been more than four, and started to sing *Al tirah, al tirah, avdi Yaakov* – Don't fear, don't fear, my servant Yaakov. I was told Old Josef just stood there, rocking back and forth, biting his lips. Then he snatched the boy back into his arms and shouted, 'God didn't help my father, and I foolishly hoped He would protect my son. So, has He?' Two months later, his wife committed suicide. Old Josef died when Yankle was sixteen, never setting foot in our schul again. An old couple, neighbors in their tenement, agreed to act as guardians of the boy until he was eighteen. So, nu, what can one expect? Yankle gets by. One helps here; another helps there."

The Rabbi closed his eyes, hoping for an inspiration. None came. *I don't think Yankle ever smiled, well, maybe at his mother's breast, but I wouldn't be surprised if she had no milk.* He looked at Yankle, at his hands, fingers curled from arthritis, discolored from age. *May he live to 120, but he looks older than my father, of blessed memory, who passed when he was ninety-six.*

"So, Yankle, I'm told you wanted to see me. I'm listening. Is there anything I can do for you? Perhaps you need help with your apartment or social services?" The Rabbi smiled. *Jewish humor: he'll tell me he needs two tickets for a Broadway musical.*

Yankle put his left hand on top of the cane and searched in the right pocket of the jacket slipping from his hunched shoulders. He took out a battered box and placed it on the table. "Here, from my father. He gave it to me when I was thirteen. 'Yakov was also called Israel, the father of our people. I have no family, only you. You should have family.'"

Yankle pulled the box apart, revealing a small brass Chai. "Next year on my birthday he explained, 'Cheit, yud – Chai, life. I kept it in the heel of my shoe when I escaped the camps and kept on walking and walking. You'd think enough walking to last two lifetimes.' I think he felt guilty about my mother. I have no family."

Yankle sighed, sat back, and pushed the box across the table towards the Rabbi with the bottom of his cane.

Rabbi Kahn stared at the box with the worn amulet, returning his gaze to Yankle. He raised an eyebrow in question.

"Please, Rabbi, I know my father would not have wanted this to end up in a museum. Maybe you know of a family that needs better mazel, or you can give it to the parents next time there's a bris, *wer weiss*, who knows?"

Yankle struggled to his feet, and the rabbi quickly rose and followed him out the door, escorting him to the schul's front entrance. He stepped out first, holding the door open. "Watch your step."

Yankle moved the cane to his left hand. "Thank you, Rabbi. Don't forget, no museum."

Rabbi Kahn thought he detected a hint of a smile as Yankle turned and continued down the steps to the sidewalk.

Paul Penske is an MFA candidate under the
mentorship of Amy Hempel at Stony Brook
University. His thesis is a collection of multi-
perspective and interconnected short stories and
vignettes set in the fictional village of Emerson, New
York. When he isn't writing, you can find him
watching twenty-year-old *Conan O'Brien* remotes,
talking to the birds outside his bedroom window, and
getting chased by his hyperactive cairn terrier. He
has been published in a handful of places.

Ode to the Firefighters of Emerson Village

At 1:02, a gray horn blared above the workbench.
Pagers beeped and whistled. Brian Blackwell's voice
echoed throughout the firehouse:

Emerson Fire Department, Signal Thirteen—
Electrical Fire. 311 Prospect Street.

Every firefighter who has ever lived (volunteer or
otherwise) has dreamed of their first big job; if they're
lucky, it might even happen within the first six months
of their career. When they heard Signal 13 (the code
for a structure fire), they immediately thought, "This
is the big job," and what they thought next was a house
with fierce orange flames dancing out every window
and thick black smoke seeping into the sky. They
thought of themselves as the hero, the person putting

out the fire. Although praying for something like this to happen might've seemed impertinent, a firefighter's first big job was an initiation into the big leagues, so to speak, and a story to tell when they're a veteran member of the fire department.

The bay doors opened. The siren on top of the firehouse cranked on, crescendoing and decrescendoing three times. Donjon, Kip, Seamus, Jaimie, and Joonior ran through the back bay door from Joe's garage to Engine 5's coat rack, where they donned their gear. Richie and Sam followed, coming down the back staircase from the upstairs kitchen. For this particular crew, it usually took them around twenty seconds each to gear up. They shimmied their legs into their bunker pants and, with their turnout coats over their shoulders and their helmets on, walked to the front of the engine to wait for a driver. In the meantime, Dave Stokes sprinted from the upstairs of the annex all the way to the chauffeur's seat and turned the engine on. He pressed the buttons that ignited the red and white lights on and around the roof, then drove the rig onto the tarmac.

The cab of Engine 5 could hold six firefighters, but only four sat in seats with SCBA air packs; the other two sat in jump seats located on either side of the cab. Kip, Seamus, Jaimie, Joonior, Richie, and Sam all climbed into the rig at the same time. They packed themselves in there like sardines. Donjon hopped into what is called the officer's seat (the front-right seat where the highest-ranking company members sit when going on a call).

30 is Signal Two, Head Chief Hank Roe said over the radio.

Another voice followed right after: "33 is Signal Two," said by Third Assistant Chief Fred Kennedy. Signal Two meant that a unit was en route to the scene.

"Oh yeah! Full house, baby!" Donjon said, looking behind him to the crew. "Let's go," he said to Dave.

"Five is Signal Two," Dave said into a walkie-talkie attached to the sun visor. He accelerated the engine onto Maple Place. A cloud of diesel smoke puffed into the bay as several cars pulled into the main parking lot with their blue lights flashing in their windshields.

Just roll an engine, Chief Roe said. The men and women who had run from the cars immediately started walking, sighing with frustration. Engine 5 turned left onto Main Street with its sirens wailing. Passersby watched as the engine roared past them, en route across town. Tourists took pictures, children covered their ears, and yet a majority of the villagers didn't seem to care, as this was only a facet of how the village itself functioned; the responding fire engine was part of downtown Emerson's daily ambience. While 5's sirens and horns ricocheted off every building and house down Main Street and up East Maron Lane, Donjon gave out assignments.

"I want St. Valentine...!" Donjon yelled over the wind waffling through the open windows.

"Roll up the windows!" Richie said from the middle seat. The only thing that was loud now was the engine compartment, which separated the front seats and the crew cab.

"I want St. Valentine and Haggard on the door in case we need to make entry!" Donjon yelled.

"You get the Hallagan tool and the axe, and I'll get the hook," Kip said to Joonior while Donjon scanned the rest of the crew.

"Campos, I want you on dry chem and walk up with me to the side of the house! Seamus, I want you to bring Blanchard and McFadden with you around the house to make sure there isn't another fire happening. I want a full perimeter sweep. Is that clear, everyone?!" Donjon asked.

"Signal 20, Captain!" the crew said in unison.

5's engines loudly inhaled as they drove up and over the hill on East Marion Lane, where they eventually turned onto Alabaster Ave. The back windows had been rolled down again, but only halfway; the wind waffled like a machine gun until the rig turned onto Terrier Street, then made a turn onto Prospect, where the rig slowed. The heavy wind turned to a gentle breeze. This neighborhood was part of Harbor Hills, known for its large waterfront houses, though this section was more suburban. Instead of mansions, there were colonials, for the most part.

311 Prospect Street was a Patriot-red, colonial revival house with a seasoned-wood panel fence on either side of the house and around the backyard. There were pine trees of various varieties standing over the house behind the property, and the grass looked like it had just been mowed a day or two prior, as the lawnmower stripes were still visible. The neighbor next door, the caller, was seen talking to a police officer near the curbline. They were standing in

front of a police interceptor. On the other side of the street were two chief cars that had responded to the call, Hank Roe and Fred Kennedy. Fred was waiting for Engine 5 to pull up in front of the house when he walked up to Donjon's window.

"Just two guys will do, Chief Roe's been talking to the homeowners," Chief Kennedy said.

"Campos with me," Donjon said as he grabbed a walkie-talkie from the center console and got out of the engine. Jaimie, who sat across from Sam in the jumper seat, went out of the cab to let Sam out, then climbed back inside. Sam grabbed the dry-chemical fire extinguisher from the hose panel transverse cabinet and walked up the lawn with Donjon.

"What's going on?" Donjon asked Chief Roe. The sidings around the breaker had burn spots. It smelled of rubber.

"We checked it out. The homeowner said they've been having issues with the breaker wires sparking. We called PPA (the Paumanok Power Authority) to see if they can come check it out and fix the issue." Fred said.

"Five is Signal 9," Donjon said into the radio.

*　*　*

"Bro, I got carded at Printing Press the other night," Richie said to Seamus inside the cab as he removed his bunker jacket. The windows had been rolled up, and the A/C system kicked on.

"No, you didn't. I don't believe you one bit," Seamus said.

"I swear to god," Richie said. "I was with Bobby and Trey."

"Did they get carded, too?" Kip asked.

"No, that's the funny thing. It was just me. I literally look older than both of them combined. They've got baby faces. I tell you, I don't think a thirty-two-year-old has ever been carded in the history of the world," Richie said.

"What happened after that?" Seamus asked.

"I think it was a new bouncer. He kept giving me a hard time, so Bobby and Trey said, 'fuck it,' and we went down to the brewery instead. I don't think I'm ever going there again," Richie said.

"Nah, we just gotta go there before the bouncer gets there," Seamus said.

"Or go in through the back door," Jaimie said.

"Richie's used to going in through the back door," Seamus quipped.

"Oh yeah, McSweeney? You should ask your mom how she likes it," Richie said. The two cackled.

Across Prospect Street, standing on the curbline, was Kurt Lynch, a tall, lanky, bespectacled man in tight-fitting pants, a blue and white-striped collared shirt, dark-brown loafers, and a comb-over hairstyle. He was trying to get insider information out of Anthony Mancuso, the village fire marshal.

"So uhh, what's going on over there?" Kurt asked. Anthony was paying too much attention across the street that he didn't even realize Kurt was talking to him. "Scuse me? Sir?"

"You talkin to me?" Anthony asked, snapping out of his gaze.

"Yes, I am. I was wondering what was going on over there," Kurt said.

"Nothing too bad, just some sparks, is all," Anthony said.

"Is that normal?" Kurt asked.

"Ehh, yeah, I guess. It could happen for a number of reasons," Anthony counted on his fingers. "One, loose wires. Two, the breaker isn't receiving enough electrical flow through the circuit. Three, the opposite, where it's overloading. Or four, the electrician did a crappy job."

"Are any of those things the reason why this is happening?" Kurt asked.

"That, my friend, I'm not too sure about. We're waiting for the power authority to show up to get some answers," Anthony said.

In his failed snooping attempt, Kurt then tried working up a conversation with one of the attractive-looking county police officers on the scene, who wasn't having any of his advances. The name on her uniform was Baxter.

"You like being a cop?" Dwayne asked.

"It's okay," Baxter nodded.

"You know, I used to know a guy on the force," Dwayne said, resting his elbow against his mailbox and crossing his right leg over his left.

"Very nice, sir," Baxter said.

"You may've known him? Officer Janeway? He was let go for some bullshit reason," Dwayne said.

"Oh... right... Officer Janeway," Baxter said, knowing full well that the person Dwayne was talking about was fired and charged for sexually assaulting several officers in his precinct a number of years ago. "Well, sir, it was nice speaking to you,"

Baxter began walking away before Dwayne asked, "Oh, wait, can I maybe get your number?"

"Sure! It's Nine-One-One, have a nice day," Baxter said.

* * *

Back at the firehouse, outside the dispatcher's office, was a counter with a TV above it that displayed the current and previous calls over the last 24 hours. A group of older men stood around it waiting in a single-file line. Next to the counter was a black box with a finger reader attached, which kept track of who showed up to calls and certain events, and ensured each member met the requirements for the Length of Service Award Program (LOSAP), which helped members gain certain retirement benefits.

At 2:01, Chief Roe radioed *Five-Two-Five* (Signal Five meant that the call was over, and Signal Two-Five meant that the units were returning to base). At the front of the line, Tom Tuten checked his watch.

"Should be any minute now," Tom said, waiting for Brian Blackwell to activate the call on the finger reader.

Behind him were Bob Meechum and his wife Debbie, and Bob Fiddich; Donnie Meyhew, James and Eoghan Strong, and probie Phil Crenshaw of Engine 5, Walton Tompkins, Captain Scottie Shaul, and probie Sal Dodge of Engine 3, Pat Tracy, John Biscotti, Hughie Wolffe, Desi Sharp, probie Bailey Roe, First Lieutenant Joe Primavera, and Second Lieutenant Matt Marcusio of Ladder One, Dale Cavanaugh and probie Candice Goldman of Engine 2, as well as veteran members Brent Coyle, Des Hanagan, Jimmy Grove, Cal Murdock, and Marty Plumm. A lot of these people came straight from work, still in their work clothes; others came in casual wear from home; and the probies had their backpacks on as they came straight from school. The finger reader beeped at 2:05, and people started to finger in. After they finished, they parted ways and went back to whatever they were doing when the call first came through.

*   *   *

After PPA came and went, Donjon got back into the officer's seat. He took his helmet off and placed it on the center console.

Joonior zoned out. The ride back from a call was always the quietest for him. While the other guys conversed about baseball or what else needed to be done for the steak night, Joonior looked out the window. When the engine drove through the three-way intersection onto Main Street, people watched and waved. Kip nudged Joonior, staring down at his helmet sitting in his lap.

"You'll get your big job, don't worry," Kip said. "I didn't get my first real big job for about a year after I joined."

"Really?"

"Uh-huh, in fact, it took me over a year to get off probation. They made me wait a few months to take the Firefighter One training out in Stewartsville so I could take it with some other fresh probies," Kip said.

"Didn't you get frustrated waiting so long for a big fire?" Joonior asked.

"Well, I think everyone gets a little antsy waiting for any call of that nature," Kip said.

"I joined thinking we'd be fighting fires like that 24/7," Joonior said.

"That's why everyone joined, my friend. But what we all learned was that fighting fires accounted for only 5% of being a firefighter, which is pretty ironic, given our job title. It's also five percent going on calls like this, or MVAs or miscellaneous calls, you know?" Kip said.

"What's the other ninety percent?" Joonior asked.

"That's in-house duties, like cleaning the rig, cleaning the tools, making everything look presentable to, not only the public, but the head honchos above us. There are also certain events running, like the steak night tonight. I'm sure there are other things I'm forgetting…"

"Cleaning the beer out of the walk-in freezer," Richie said on the other side of Kip.

"Oh, right, that's an important one. That also helps the bevy every time we have a new event," Kip said.

"Supporting local businesses," Seamus said before the cab laughed.

"All this right now, what just happened, is part of it too," Kip continued. "That ninety percent is what keeps the firehouse alive. So, don't sweat over not getting your first big job; it all comes with time."

R. P. Singletary writes across genres, hails from the rural southeastern U.S., and dabbles in other media, some of which appear on www.rpsingletary.com or elsewhere socially (youtube too) via @rpsingletary. Affiliations include Dramatists Guild & Authors Guild. Thank you.

A. Windfall

People need understanding more than a good night's
rest or a decent day job.

Maybe even more than decent food. Water, we all
know—those on land cannot live on water alone.

The man's résumé read one word long, but it should've
been a whole paragraph shorter under my discernment.
Let's call him Bob— The young fella had only lived
in one state, not a big one at that, which I won't
partition by voiced appellation (we all know how they,
those from there, are prone to pride). I used to be one
of them myself, and no, not from there as they, mighty
proud, are wont to remind all of us lowered

transplants. I won't share if she, my wife, may be from there either, but yes, I shall say the pair of us both rightly know folks *from* there and *of* there, humans almost exacting approximate the familiar stranger of a man sitting before me, his clockwork of entry unfortunate, two blessed blinks prior to my second blackened sip.

"Yes, sir, an early riser, been such all my life, yes sir, yes sir," he said before judging me, *sir*. "Don't go for coffee, not at all, even after a night of—"

"Early riser," I muttered in between my next two swallows. A lost bird, missing its own paired half, half of the globe too by that late month brutal, avian by the same name, rapped itself against the wintry window at that very *tok* of *tik*. Warming a warning, I eyed the hearth, the office corner cold.

"Antique guns...." He recast himself, which I juried an improvement. "...ones that work, those look to be." Steering the conversation back into simple sentiment germane to our environs, he commented on arms and ammunition clinging to the dusty, clouded boards of the room's interior wall.

To accomplish a necessary task, one must convey a certain redeeming sense of well-timed usefulness, alms alimentary or oblation otherwise obligated. On that, the ineffable man has already done more for me. As if a lowly pilgrim amid an incensed priest commanding a strange ritual in a distant temple, he kept eyeing the chilled air between us, the parted steam wandering above my thick mug, its shotgun handle barely taped, it rendering firm all three of us salvation seekers.

"I like guns though," the man added, "been around 'em all my life. Eyes rammed shut inside my head, hands cut and tied behind my belt, I, I know the difference between a...."

In my old and childless age, I had of late quit many of my younger games, gave up cold river fishing last season when my right knee went somewhere to find my left one around an elbow bandaged, burdened the last few weeks especially by the joker windowpane reflecting my holy sock of self, imprisoned once-wild spirit sadly shuffling indoors, saggy half-spent and near to nothing, almost again unuseful on a floor uncleaned and also in mock. Wet rag me, tamed but for my foulest humor of old-codger utterances. In these ridiculous interviews, urged to salvage a croaking business, these hours I dared not laugh and waste what, anything. A latent muscle's penultimate memory of energetic movement eternal? No, not about to lapse and let this fool in on a good one at my own final expense. I chuckled at my off-leaning head talk, self-censoring before tongue grew toes. He didn't flinch, but shifted his gaze, wicking up all the wildlife wonders, trophies of plumage and hide, twofold, brassy and weathered. Frankly, I didn't fathom the lecture going in his direction. He did know about guns. He sapped on and on. I drank until I was full. Or cup and pot both empty, doctor's orders no seconds. Good thing I already knew my decision. This boy is not gonna waste more than five minutes of this geezer's remainder, regardless of who his fine peeps might turn out to be, if he lasts long enough for it to matter. Senior sage, teenage me, *teeter*-tooter.

"Never lived another place, eh?" I said, fiddling with papers and pencils spread across my immigrant grandfather's worn lawyer desk.

The man reached for the side of his burnt face. When the secretary brought him in, I was standing by the fire and saw where he'd missed a whisker's swipe across his swarthy dewlap. That spot he now rubbed, like a loose-set clamp on a genie lamp.

"Makes not a f-*lick* of difference, son, any more we got youngins from all over here, back East, down South, overseas, hell I never know'd some of 'em places existed 'til men started sendin' in these damn applications."

I waved my free hand across the mess of my business board. The man quit his wishing for a wash or a windfall and put his hand back on his thigh. I noticed the new suit, totally inappropriate for the line of work he'd applied for. I gave him two points for ridiculousness. Another single for the half-ironed shirt, minus ½ of that one for a ketchup stain on the shiny tie sporting the store tag. The secretary said he called in a rush early, asked not where to eat come morning, but also where to buy a tie that early in town. I believe he'd been to the diner. Good and godly, mine. My brother over at the general store texted me about the tie, saying, "won't believe this one, he put it on *before* he bought it or tried to even with the mirror looked like he was wranglin a boar to cauterize new clerk had to assist please hire po bo asap."

"Well, what do you say, sir, I don't mean to be overbold, sir, just to show polite initiative, sir, do I get the—"

Hy-aaack. The light smoke from the fireplace ignited a painful memory of a lung's legacy. I found some phlegm to fuss over in my esophagus. I was still happy I'd quit an awful habit when I did. *Hy-aaack.* A hot rainbow landed in the wastebasket. Thank God my brother stopped texting those silly smiley symbols, goddamn.

"Good shot," the boy said.

Yeah, initiative all right, bordering on ballsy for a fool with no kin in these parts. Or kith to kick it with. No references, not a damn one.

"You remind me of some men I once...."

The man leaned forward, elbows on his thighs, as if around a campfire. I heard something rip. He eased up and eerily looked at the crackling fire.

"Do ya type?"

Without knocking, the secretary brought in two more logs and threw them on the fire.

"Well?" I repeated, while we two stared at the third person in the room.

The secretary stoked the burning, playing with the new guy, right on cue, like yesterday with the other one, scared off before an offer never in the works.

"I always say some skills never go out of fashion." I cleared my throat. "Give me a typewriter, not a keyboard. A pencil, not a mouse—"

"Yes, sir, I do."

"But can you hunt?"

The wise youth wanted to think about this one, which gave me my day's political answer, but truth be told I'd already made up my mind months ago the hour his letter arrived, no email as so many, but a plain white letter, a single first-class stamp with the simple flag in the perfect place, respectful, envelope and letter too typed neat and old school on an aged machine begging better ribbon, he a cheap soul but

sound specimen we could mold in this dying business
he didn't yet figure he'd end up inheriting if he could
help me keep it alive, hence the reason I reckoned best
what to do upon sudden apparition, his lonely letter
courtesy USPS arriving on my birthday, church being
twenty-four after: all souls' or saints' dependent on
one's choosing.

Poetry

K.L. Johnston is an award-winning author, photographer, and poet best known for works centered in spiritual experience, nature, and trauma survival. Author of three books of poetry, *In Every Season*, *The Nature of These Gifts*, and *Grace Period*, her works have appeared in more than fifty literary magazines and anthologies. A retired antiques and art dealer she currently lives near the Savannah River. You can find out more at www.Facebook.com/Kathleen-Johnston or visit her online gallery at 1-kathleen-johnston.pixels.com.

No Goodbye

I never saw my father's face in death.

I'm glad.

My sister said

it looked like some old geezer

had stolen his clothes

then worn them to bed.

Now when I want to ask his advice,

he's just stepped out:

he's hilling up the potatoes,

or chopping wood or

he's sitting at his desk,

book in hand, mulling over the Reformation.

Knowing him, he could be up to some mischief

to make my mother laugh

or working a deal

to bring up to the troops

the best malted batch of the angel's share.

I know he is busy now.

Generally I know what advice he would give me

from among the blessed.

And the knowledge of these things would be
obscured

without the gift of a closed coffin.

previously published in. In Every Season,
Westbow Press. 2020.

Small Bouquets

I.

Lady banks roses hang

over the front porch,

toss down their petals,

welcoming a bride

or a hero. Buds

of something fragile

and long forgotten

begin unfurling

as I step inside.

II.

My heart lifts.

Unknowing,

my parents

shared their gift:

unveiling

her face in

delight as

he handed

her flowers.

III.

When he brought the vegetables

in from the garden

his hardened hands also brought

gardenias for Mom,

daisy mums for me: bright gifts,

fresher nourishment.

previously published in the Closed Eye Open
Maya's Micros, Batch 22, August 2021.

Sharon E. Ludan holds a B.A. from the College of New Jersey and an M.S. from Boston University. As an American diplomat, Ludan has lived and worked in many countries throughout the world. Her work has been published by *Proverse Hong Kong, Wingless Dreamer*, Quillkeepers Press, Unleash Press; the *Kansai Scene*; the *OSIPP Journal*, and elsewhere. Sharon hopes you enjoy these poems!

The Mole

Searching napes of necks

unknowing

what it was I sought

thereon:

half-forgotten dream

revived

in the meeting of

your mole.

Shaded cool

in thick brown hair

lifting to smoothness

and oh, soft nape!

Where watched my fate

in the eye of your mole.

Procreation

A naked body

is warm

to the touch;

easily slips

from caress to lust.

Primordial urgence

pressing flesh

to flesh,

two souls

entwined

in the dance of love.

Energies surging

higher, deeper,

converging,

merging,

two become one...

Then Flash!

Bang!

Fusion explosion

cracks the universe

splits —

emits a new soul.

Two become three:

the eternal

mystery

of procreation.

Nancy Lubarsky, a retired NJ school superintendent, holds a doctorate in English Education. She has been published in various journals including *Exit 13*, *Lips*, *Tiferet*, *Poetic*, *Stillwater Review* and *Paterson Literary Review*. Nancy is the author of three books: *Tattoos* (Finishing Line), *The Only Proof* (Kelsay Press), and her latest book, *Truth to the Rumors* (Kelsay Press), a finalist for the 2023 Laura Boss Narrative Poetry Award. Her poetry/film collaboration, *The Mess* (with Sophia Cansalvo) won first place this year in the Moving Words Showcase. She was also selected to participate in Poetry X Hunger, where poets combat food insecurity with hands-on experiences and poetic responses. Both

projects were sponsored by Arts by the People. A
lifelong New Jerseyan, Nancy lives in Cranford with
her husband and dog, Penny.

Work Clothes

[for my father]

Long after you were gone

I found your cuff links

in a velvet pouch among my

bracelets. The A (for Arthur) etched

in gold ovals, leaned right, the tail

swirled left, like a wave receding.

There's mystery in the curls,

from a time before font names

were familiar, when elaborate letters

pledged stories to come.

I never saw you wear them—never

watched you twist the levers into slits

on cuffed shirts, or slip your arm into

the sleeve of a pinstriped suit.

Your work clothes were heavy twill—

drawstring pants, an apron—

you left at midnight with them

stashed in a canvas sack, and headed

deep into the Bronx.

Over time, they wore and frayed,

stained with jelly and chocolate.

In middle school, after Home Ec

ended, you surprised me with the

sewing machine. In late afternoon,

at the dinette, you cut patches

while I mended holes and edges.

My toe touched the pedal, the machine

whirred—you asked me to print

your initials inside along the seams.

previously published in Paterson Literary Review

Maestro

[after Maestro, the movi])

My father was no Leonard

Bernstein. He never sang, or

played an instrument, never lived

in a luxury apartment, or hosted

elite dinner parties. Bernstein was

trim and fashionable—my father,

overweight and scruffy. But they

both were born and died in the same

years. Both were Jews who grew up

in safe New York at a time when so

many were murdered elsewhere. In

the evenings, Bernstein, at Carnegie

Hall, raised his baton to the strings, the

horns, the woodwinds. As sweet music

merged and swelled, the audience roared

Bravo, Bravo! Meanwhile, my father,

a Bronx baker, pointed at shelves, yelled

to porters for supplies that were blended

at the precise temperatures, times and

amounts, so each cake and cookie melded

and rose into a luscious confection. In

the morning, he'd hear the customers (who

nibbled on samples from the counter),

Oy, so delicious! How does he do it?

previously published in Tiferet Magazine

What If, As Your Sister Claimed

[for My Fathe]

A thing may happen and be a total lie; another thing
may not happen and be truer than the truth

    — Tim O'Brien, The Things They Carried

What if you were never on that battleship, as

your sister claimed, when she heard your voice

on the tape I mailed to her after your funeral?

What if you never went to the latrine—there

was no explosion, no friends left behind on

the deck, no shrapnel in your leg? What if

you hadn't spent months in a hospital, tending

the gash that she argued was from an accident

in your father's bakery? What if there was

no purple heart —you didn't give it away to

a stranger? That day we talked for hours; I

recorded it all. Years later, my friend asked

if I was curious about what really happened,

but I already knew. It was a war story.

Michele Harvey is a poet whose work has appeared
in several literary journals including: *Progenitor,
Copper Nickel,* and *The Litchfield Review.*

Finding You

[for my father]

I felt you in that butterfly

one October morning near the lake.

I recognized your wryness,

frail monarch in flight,

nearly landing on my breakfast.

When I was little, you flitted away,

lured by work.

I fluttered like a moth,

lost among the scent

of your empty, waiting clothes.

But now, adorned by offerings

released by you to play on wings,

I understand with nourished eyes,

the comfort of my leisure

is all you sought.

Moved by your means,

our ties transcend location.

Your gift to me is found;

in finally finding you.

previously published in,
Poetry for Living an Inspired Life

The Sign of Cancer

[for my father]

Your birthday does not end with you.

Summer oozes from the grill,

but birds still sing in rounds.

I celebrate your life beyond

where sky and earth connect.

Here, in the gloaming heat,

my memories bear no sacrifice,

and by supper's end, one large bite

of your birthday cake remains.

I watch as swallows swoop

to taste the frosted flowers cleaving to my plate,

but soon they fly off toward the summer moon,

ruled by cancer's throne.

I suspect this is where you've gone.

And this is where you wait.

For you are never one who passes on dessert,

unless you started learning late.

previously published in Poetry for Living an Inspired Life

Veronica Tucker is an emergency medicine and addiction medicine physician, mother of three, and lifelong New Englander. Her poetry explores the intersections of medicine, motherhood, memory, and being human. Her work appears in *One Art, Eunoia Review, Berlin Literary Review*, and in *The Book of Jobs* anthology. She shares more at veronicatuckerwrites.com and on Instagram @veronicatuckerwrites.

The House He Holds

He wakes as a stay-at-home dad,

before the children stir,

before the dogs circle the kitchen,

before the day asks for more

than one man should have to give.

He packs lunches,

sets shoes in neat pairs,

waits with open hands

for a toddler's small trust,

for the older two to grumble awake.

The house bends toward him,

toward the one who keeps

the rhythm of breakfasts and backpacks,

the leash loops,

the steady ground that allows me

to walk into chaos and return whole.

Some heroes carry stethoscopes.

His cape is a dish towel

draped over one shoulder.

The Sharp Tongue and the Pen

You taught me medicine

was never only sutures and scans,

but words,

how they could cut or cure.

In the trauma bay, you were fearless,

your wit a scalpel that spared nothing,

yet you guarded the fragile thing in me

that wanted to write,

to place language beside pulse.

I remember you leaning at the desk,

chart notes scattered like loose pages,

telling me to keep a notebook close,

because medicine fades without memory.

You never asked me to choose.

Instead, you told me

that a physician who listens

might also be a poet,

that both require silence first.

The pages I blacken now

still carry your voice,

sharp, unyielding,

yet never unkind.

My Brother, the Test Pilot

He has flown into skies

I can only imagine,

measured his life in takeoffs and landings,

risk stitched into every calculation.

Retired now, he carries the quiet

of someone who has tested gravity

and returned.

Montreal snow rests on his shoulders,

a border between us,

yet the bond remains familiar as breath.

I remember the hangar smell of fuel

that clung to his jacket,

the way he spoke of speed

as if it were a language,

and I remember him now,

still steady, still my brother,

his laughter a compass

that finds me wherever I stand.

Among the Men in Medicine

In the bright wash of the emergency lights,

I have worked beside men

who steady a gurney with one hand,

chart with the other,

and still find space for a joke

that cracks the room open.

They carry stretchers,

carry silence,

carry the weight of families

who ask for miracles.

I think of the nurse who whispered

a line from a song during a code,

just loud enough for me to hear,

or the tech who caught my eye

before I spoke hard news,

sharing the weight without words.

Not all heroes announce themselves.

Some wear scrubs that smell of bleach

and keep going,

not for glory,

but because someone has to.

Copper in the Palm

My father carried laughter like loose change,

ready to spend on whoever needed it.

He could turn a silence into a story,

a sidewalk into a marketplace,

a pocket of pennies into proof

that nothing small should be forgotten.

He lived as if time were a sale

you had to talk your way into,

all charm and bargain,

never leaving without more friends

than when he arrived.

Now I keep his ring,

its worn edge pressing into my hand,

a reminder that presence

does not vanish,

it only changes form.

David Radavich has published a variety of poetry, drama, essays, and reviews. His plays have been performed across the U.S. and in Europe. His latest books are _UNTER DER SONNE / UNDER THE SUN: German Poems_ (Deutscher Lyrik, 2021) and _HERE'S PLENTY_ (Cervena Barva, 2023).

Mansmell

It's what attracts men

to the locker-room,

that aroma of sweat

and testosterone,

testimony to masculine

achievement and camaraderie,

safe space like
no other,

where one can be

naked

and unguarded,

free to soap

and lather

and rinse

to a clean sheen

as if we

won the game.

.

Doyle-Gillespie is a Baltimore City poet and writer. He holds a BA in History from George Washington University, and a Master of Liberal Arts from Johns Hopkins University. His poems are drawn from his world travel, and his work in education, and law enforcement. These poems represent his fascination with history and culture, and how those forces play roles in the most intimate parts of our lives. His books of poetry include _Masala Tea and Oranges, On the Later Addition of Sancho Panza, Socorro Prophecy, Gentrifying the Plague House,_ and _Aerial Act_. His most recent title is _Father of the Red Grotto Used Bookstore_. He holds a BA in History from George Washington University, and a Master of Liberal Arts from Johns Hopkins University. This

year, he was first-place grand-prize winner of the
Iridescence Award, the third-place winner of the
African Diaspora Award 2024, the third-place winner
of the Westmoreland Arts and Heritage Festival, and
an honourable mention in the Rhonda Gail Williford
award for poetry.

But, His Clothing is Still There

When time has ripened

and the day's dying light

is in your favor,

find the key to his armoire.

Stand just so for the gloaming glow

of the waning day

in mother's full-length mirror.

Try on his abandoned tweed,

segregation's scent still

in the weave.

Pull his braces up with your thumbs

and let them snap down

on your narrow collar-bone shoulders.

Tones of his lone saxophone recital

at a brown-bag club

will resonate in your ears.

Give his fedora a try.

Lower the brim to hide your eyes.

Go look through the blinds

at the dying light to see

how the sundown town shadows

take their own sweet time

to recede.

Mike Everley has been writing for many years and has had poetry, short stories and articles published in numerous publications and online. He was a member of both the NUJ and the Society of Authors before retirement. Now, a silver scribbler, he devotes his time to creative writing.

The Last Post

High on the mountainside

near the Guardian's[1]

rusty metal pride

Brynithel Cemetery

stretches marbled rows

of engraved memories

under the morning sun.

A sole bugler plays

haunting the still air.

We stand heads bowed

beside my uncle's grave.

Safe in an armoured shell

---

[1] The Guardian Of The Valleys is a tall statue overlooking the landscaped former Six Bells Colliery site where in 1960 an underground explosion killed 45 miners. The Guardian is made from thick weathering steel, which allows a protective rust to form on its surface.

through Caen's wreckage,

Falaise's devastation

and across the Rhine

he survived.

But this last battle

was too much.

Hardly able to walk

fed with oxygen

from a mask

he clung to life.

Now we stand beside

his open grave

as silence falls

deep and dark as night.

Pete Mullineaux grew up in the UK and now lives in Galway, Ireland. He's published five collections, most recently _We are the Walrus_ (Salmon 2022) which was featured on the cover of the World Wildlife Fund's *The Circle Magazine*. His environmental poetry film *Careful what you wish for orang-utan*' won the 2023 Home-stage Poetry Competition (UK).

Slides

1

Before I could swim in the deep

end of the pool, at the bottom

of the big slide, the top half

of my father bobbed in the

water, arms outstretched

ready to catch me;

which he did

every time.

2

At home we had a stair banister

overburdened with coats

which were always

falling on the floor:

school mornings

he'd pick them

up, car engine

running –

out of his depth.

previously published in A Father's Day,
Salmon Poetry 2008

Possibly a Poem about Patriarchy

This came from a dream...

we fathers have arrived to pick up our kids

from playschool...

      to find the building on fire, flames raging —

      we're told

not to enter, the burning roof about to collapse —

      but each man hears an inner voice

      commanding, "Save your child!" and so

we dash in, search frantically around,desperately

calling out names, but with

falling timbers, the smoke and the confusion of

bodies crashing into one another, it's

seemingly hopeless, until

a different voice speaks to all at once: "You have just

a few precious

seconds; rescue one child, *any* child"...

so each grabs the nearest one

and escapes

      not a moment

or another ten thousand years

to spare...

previously published in We are the Walrus,
Salmon Poetry 2022

Emma Kennedy is a teacher and Masters Degree student with a love for writing poems.

The Deer in Burghley Park

To one especially, I got close.

Whilst to most,

there's too much fear;

before running to safety elsewhere.

It was unsafe, gazing.

I took a million pictures of The Stag

and zoomed in on his coat:

stunning. Against the Earth and sky.

I bought a pot of tea at The Orangery

and took the last train home.

Alone. As always these days.

Except, memories are like photographs

and he is still there, looking back.

I've realised I had forgotten

how wild he was.

Free at last.

How wild he was.

I cropped the photos of the stag.

Cool and calm. Relaxed.

I airbrushed many of myself.

I'm not like him.

My hair has grown dark at the roots again.

It's long and maybe wild.

Sometimes I kid myself

and I believe

I'm free at last as well.

Crumpled Roses—

A poem about Valentine's Day

I bought some paper flowers once from a market stall;
    near London's Covent Garden in The West End
    where all the best voices are heard.
    They were overpriced
    but beautiful, blossoming, plastic fakes.
    I loved them.
    I had never had the flowers I wanted:
    a brightly coloured bunch
    with thorns and leaves and fir cones from a
    dreamy, loving boyfriend.
    Handsome and clever and kind. And funny, like me!
    He had bought them on his way home from work.
Usually on Valentine's Day,
    I do something else instead:
    I'm a swimmer, a singer, a runner, a writer... I
    enjoy life completely....
    and do everything I can;
    which is enough, for me, anyway. And so, this year,
    I will happily open
    my clean, wooden box
    and take out a pretty floral bag.
I will wear my favourite perfume from Neal's Yard.
    And I'll display, again,
the same old, crumpled roses.

Shaquille Mendes, has always played sports, starting
with baseball _ T-ball when he was 5. He had an
older brother that was already playing the sport. The
three he enjoyed most were Baseball, Basketball, &
Football. The sports were mainly played locally
while also traveling for All-Star games and
Tournaments as well. Shaq stopped playing in High
School his Sophmore Year after becoming a Father.
Baseball was played at the following: Dias Field,
Southend (Lot13), Brooklawn Park, & Voc-Tech.
Basketball was played at the following: Boy's &
Girls Club of New Bedford, B.B.A Dartmouth Ma,
Buttonwood Park, Magnet Park, Ashely Park,

Hazelwood Park, C.Y.O., Y.M.C.A. of New Bedford,
& Voc-Tech. Football was Played at the following:
D.Y.A.A back baseball field, Voc-Tech(fresh.), New
Bedford High(soph.) *They also were outside weekly
though. Playing neighborhood pickup games behind
the local Highschool, Public Basketball Courts, &
Baseball fields*(No first baseman or right fielder so
a hit that way was an out. Hahaha...) Baseball ages ;
5 – 15 Basketball ages ; 7 – 16 Football ages ; 7 – 16
Shaq.

Hey Coach;
Thank you,

Not one in specific, but all of them, Baseball,
Football & Basketball. Each one brought with
them lessons, values & built bonds. Each and every
practice, hardworking individuals pushing to
achieve one goal.

That was:

WIN...

Thanks for showing me how to block the son
with my glove Thanks for showing me how to
block their son on the offensive line

Thanks for showing me how to block their son
by jumping high...

Thanks for giving us your time—

Time that you coulda spent at home, with your
family especially with your kids.

Although; we were such too..

Thanks for showing me how to read the signs &
at the same time be alert of fake signals *[ear
tug]*

Thanks for showing me how to stand & at the
same time when I'd fall you'd say get back up
Thanks for showing me what it means to hustle
& at the same time be patient...

Thanks for being out there with us, Sweating like
us— but not running

Getting wet like us— using an umbrella tho
Cheering for us— your're our fans too...

Hey Coach, I'm sorry.

I never gave up but we didn't win every time, you
showed me how to deal with loss while still being
a Winner lesson learned.

I'm sorry. I wasn't present for that trip to Gillette,
but we had plenty bus rides had you feeling like a
student again.

I'm sorry. I didn't complete the task that you had
asked, I wasn't vocal

enough now may voice be heard.

On the Diamond, The Field, & The Courts
Coaches—Teammates— Fans

I cal I that a Tri-Fecta...

Peers— Guidance— Mentors That's a Dad...

Hey Coaches ,

I remember each and every one of you...

The colors we worn, the games we lost, the times
ya'll yelled, not only at us but at the Refs &
Umps— you know the times

Ya'll had our backs. The coins for the canteen, the
challenges *"Complete this get a water break"*.
The competiveness you instilled in us. The pride
ya'll showed when we—

Crossed the plate, Found the End-zone & Knocked
down a 3.

The hugs, the high fives, the early morning
Saturday practices.

Nothing was better then : them end of the year
gatherings...

Hey Coach , thanks for showing me life is more
then what is in a Stat Column...

Edward Heathman grew up in South Wales. He has had writing published in *The Manchester Review, The Manchester Anthology, The Visual-Verse Anthology, Poetry Wales, the Bluebird Anthology, and on Ink, Sweat & Tears*. He lives in Stockport, and in his spare time, runs a YouTube channel, *Gagging4Lit*, where he talks about books. Thank you for taking the time to read my work.

My Own Private Idaho

[For Gabriel]

In this one   Keanu Reeves is carrying me   and
my   narcoleptic body

exactly as the director wants —   roadside   away
from the broken-down

motorbike   we are   meant to have dragged
ourselves on

all the way from   somewhere   like Oregon   or
Seattle,   someplace lacking

in A listers   and easy enough   to disappear in.
I am performing

my tiredness so well   I am a winter tree
leftover to spring fields.

I want it to be hard   to fall asleep,   for it to feel
earned.   I want it

to be like Marilyn Monroe   running   her
lines again in her audition

for The Asphalt Jungle,   so awfully frantic   to
be taken seriously

for the part,   the squeeze   of a chance
gold-trophied   comeback

But it's so painless,   giving in   to his dependable
forearms   his strong heart.

To be taken seriously   is to lie   right down
in front of everyone

and allow yourself   to falter   and wake   to
the unforgiving sun

in the emptying   sky, dead grass   under your
head,   the sly-sweet smell

of petrol.   The definitive   clapboard   of
shame.   Nothing

like a disaster to get people's attention.
They found a road

that undulated in just   the right way   for
the shot,   that really

went on   for-fucking-ever. You   know,   they had
to keep relighting the fire

in the scene where I said,   I love you   and
you don't pay me.

I couldn't wash my face or touch my hair.   At
twenty-three

I will never again be   so beautiful,   so willing
to take my clothes off

as I am with him: the man   in the black
leather jacket he switched for a suit,

who said   he wouldn't   sell me while I slept
(and I believed him).

Five more minutes,   please.   Can we run that
one   more   time

before   he   sets me down   into   another
heavying drift.

Allen Braden is the author of <u>A Wreath of Down and Drops of Blood</u>, a finalist for the Walt Whitman Award judged by Mary Oliver, and Elegy in the Passive Voice, winner of the University of Alaska's Midnight Sun Chapbook Contest. His poems have been anthologized in *The Bedford Introduction to Literature, Poetry: An Introduction, Thinking and Writing about Poetry, Best New Poets, Spreading the Word: Editors on Poetry, Cascadia Field Guide, Dear Human at the Edge of Time: Poems on Climate Change in the United States, Attached to the Living World: A New Ecopoetry Anthology and The World Is Charged: Poetic Engagements with Gerard Manley Hopkins.*

Grinding Grain

The belt, tight as a razor strop,

whips from tractor to hammer mill

and scares out of our grain bin an owl.

Welded pipe coughs flour into bags

stenciled *H & H* or *Logan's Feed & Seed*.

I take another off my father's hands,

another cinched with his square knot

better than any I used to tie.

Easily, I buck those bags onto the stack

that shoulders the granary wall.

The air thickens this morning light

sifting around the blurred belt.

When I turn back, he's gone

inside a cloudbank of flour

the way burlap can swallow

so many pounds of ground durum.

All our lives, we work this way.

He sacks and ties.

I lift and stack.

Our bodies slowly growing white.

previously published in Elegy in the Passive Voice
(University of Alaska/Fairbanks)

Sally Mills graduated as an artist and went on to pursue a career devoted to nature conservation. She has written/illustrated three publications: her debut memoir, <u>Island to Island</u>, and accompanying Photograph Collection, together with the production of illustrations for a children's book, <u>*Boomy the Bittern*</u>. With a drive and motivation to inspire people about nature and our role within it, she has become captivated by the world of poetry. She has had children's poems published by the Dirigible Balloon and has recently had poems selected by *The Toy and Little Thought Press* magazines. Her poetry for adults is due to appear in four anthologies.

Dad

growing sunflowers

ten foot tall
guiding me
from when I was small

tennis on the lawn
podding broad beans
going for walks
pooh sticks in streams

singing songs
making up words
sharing my passion
for wildlife and birds

learning to drive
always had time
to talk and hear of
stuff on my mind

David Ram's recent poems appear in numerous
magazines and anthologies, including *Amethyst
Review, Gargoyle Magazine, Stone Poetry Quarterly,
The Orchards Poetry Journal, Unearthed*, and
elsewhere. He retired from teaching community
college and lives with his wife in western
Massachusetts, where he practices writing, rowing,
and grandparenting.

My Kids Know a Flathead from a Phillips

At the cellar bench, you'd say, "Hold the light."

Though at first I didn't get why, I stood

beside you learning how to fix and build,

to handle tools, read a spirit level,

decide what's plumb and true. To measure twice

to a sixteenth or eyeball it and let

it rip. Not only see but hear and feel

just how forgiving or unyielding some

matter can be. Apply force or allow

mystery oil to work. Most important,

when anyone extends an open hand,

place in it what they need before they ask.

As ever, Dad, with grandkids of my own,

I am practicing still to hold that light.

previously published in Living Our Blessings:
Aging, Mortality and Gratitude (2025)

I Only Did the Head

Remember going down cellar to crank

the old-school, metal Boston sharpener?

I would drag a dull number 2 along

the wall, holding steady my arm and hand,

and let my descending body's motion

control the sweeping shapes of pencil marks.

Over time, a duck's silhouette transformed

into the sketch of a huge waterfowl

dabbling playfully across the stairwell.

Dad discovered the drawing, erupted,

lined us all up and demanded to know

who did it. We studied our shoes, he pledged

escalating penalties, then six eyes

turned on me. *"I confess. I only did*

the head." Laughter clinched his prosecution.

You three witnesses slunk away while I

was held for sentencing. He threw the book

at me, *How to Draw Figures & Faces,*

and piled on years of pastels and vellum,

cool and unusual punishment for life.

previously published in Living Our Blessings:
Aging, Mortality and Gratitude (2025)

Peter Devonald is Pushcart, Forward Prize and twice Best Of The Net nominated poet who is published in hundreds of journals including *Broken Sleep*, six Broken Spine anthologies, *Abridged, Alchemy Spoon, Dreich and London Grip*. Winner Broken Spine Readers' Choice Award 2025, Loft Books 2024, Waltham Forest, FofHCS, two HoH's, runner-up Shelley Memorial and N2tS 2024, Finalist Tickled Pink, commended *Bermondsey and Beyond, Poetry Café, Hippocrates, Passionfruit Review* and *Allingham*. Children's Bafta nominated.

Uneducated Me

The world passes me by, as the swifts above,
my nose is blocked with chronic disease,
my clothes are old and past their best,
my hair is wild and impossible and free,
I watch the world distant as a dream.

I love more than anything to be seen,
but remain hidden, behind closed doors, mostly.
I believe in the arts and literature, but barely read,
except the lines of pity written all over your face;
I rattle with regrets and tablets, I churn inside.

I learned my place with all the flowers flourishing,
all deep regrets, all whispers of being a barbarian,
a liar, chauvinist and voyeuristic masculinity; I am
football, cricket, beer and whisky. I am a role, an
exercise in futility, an anachronism, a cliché, a man.

I am unaware of the modern world, too old now
to change my ways, too old to realise the importance
of pronouns, positive discrimination beyond equality,
out of time, out of place, out of step, an outsider, still I
try my best, a recollection, past tense, an act of kindness.

Cody Draco is an emerging queer poet, settled but never stagnant, creatively restless in the rural sanctuary of southern Kentucky, United States. His poem,"Anatomy of the Human Experience",was selected as the winner of the 2025 Chaffin/Kash Prize which is presented annually by the Kentucky State Poetry Society. His collection,"Spirit of the Cowboy", was awarded the Voyages of Verses Book Award by OneTribune. His work carves through raw emotional terrain, wielding sharp societal critique, surreal imagery, and language bent to his will. Unflinching yet deeply human, his poetry pushes boundaries while distilling meaning from the void of 21st-century existence in an intentional effort to code a new masculinity.

Dumpster Fire

the first day we met

he dove headfirst into a dumpster fire

sorted through the spiritual debris

and resuscitated my disposed-of body

it may sound strange to you

but I've never felt more supported

then while lying there in a state of

pause on the cracked concrete

surrounded by useless scraps of my former self

all of the self-doubts he pulled

out and threw onto the ground

in a valiant effort to assist me

now securely fastened

in the sturdy stretcher of his arms

I have no clue where he will take me

but I know this for certain

it will be the one place I ever belong

Keith Gaboury earned an MFA in Creative Writing from Emerson College. The Pedestrian Press published _Oakland, I'm Not Dead_ in 2020, Kelsay Books published _The Cosmos is Alive_ in 2023, and Falkenberg Press published Still Human in 2025. Monetized Happiness is forthcoming from American Poetry Systems. Keith lives in Oakland, California. Learn more at <u>keithgaboury.com</u> and <u>keithgaboury.me</u>.

Fatherhood Growing

The first time I lied to our daughter, I declared,
you can do whatever a man does. Words shot out
like a pressurized sprinkler onto her freshly
formed frame.

The second time I lied, I spat out, *he didn't mean
to hit you.* Words morphed into American-made
bullets.

The third time I lied, I whispered, *I will always
tell you the truth, my love.* Words still like a
stillborn life.

Jarvis Ottum writes middle-grade horror. His favorite authors are R.L. Stine and Stephen King. His poem 'Wicked' appears in the anthology *Balm: Poetry for Beautiful Broken Souls*. His works have also appeared on *Agape Review*, LinkedIn, TripAdvisor, and the *Uvalde Leader* newspaper. (P.S. He's also a correction officer)

Correction's Officer Pledge

I vow to back the GRAY

of the

Torres Ney Complex

And the

Texas Department of Criminal Justice!

A Family

United

Unbreakable

With Integrity

And

Professionalism for all.

Jawn Van Jacobs is a rock n roll poet, myth-maker and hedge-walker. His work has appeared in *Cool Beans Lit*, *Witches Magazine*, *Moonday Magazine*, and *Paper Dragon*. This rock n roll poet lights up raw narratives imbued with sex, drugs and the occult; shedding light on the lives of those living on the hedges of society. His debut chapbook, <u>bastard bee</u>, was published by Finishing Line Press in August 2025.

Johnny the Witch

his name is my name too—

who come from cunning mountain men,

who wear antlers when the moon is full

to run barefoot over the wet wool moss.

but our blood has been rained down

over centuries, men have strayed from nature—

many of us now, veer left into witch trials

for refusing to cut out our tongues—

making us hung in more ways than one.

still we can catch serpents with our bare hands

& stay blasé between rounds of buckshot—

with red-tails circling wherever we trail

as we pass through snowflakes & spiderwebs—

friend to animals, enemy of all-rulers.

Linda M. Crate (she/her) is a Pennsylvanian writer whose poetry, short stories, articles, and reviews have been published in a myriad of magazines both online and in print. She has fifteen published chapbooks the latest being: <u>not your piñata</u> (Alien Buddha Publishing, June 2025).

my great uncle jim

loves history
and telling stories
of growing up and the
people he knew,

when i was little
my mother and i
used to live with him
and my gran;

he would always tell
me to tell gran
to take a chill pill—

likes to be silly
and make others laugh,
he gave me the nickname
typing tilly one summer
and my little sister was
called apple annie because
she loved to eat apples;

but she didn't care
for that much—

he told me when i was one
i went running towards the lake,
and he he had to scoop me up;

i always admired his knowledge
and his wisdom—

love hearing his stories
about aunt alice
or any of his adventures growing
up because it was a different
time from what i know now,

and i will always treasure
every laugh or smile he gives me.

silence can be golden

uncle john is

shy like

me,

never expects

me to talk unless

i want to;

and i admire his

endless

creativity—

his pictures

are always

gorgeous,

and sometimes i am

jealous of his ability to

always get the perfect photograph;

but maybe it's because i always

see the finished and polished product

and not the failures in between because

practice makes progress—

but he's kind and funny,

a reflective person who understands

silence can be golden;

and i can appreciate someone

who lets me approach

the world with whimsy and wonder

and curiosity.

Lani T. is a 23-year-old writer from Sicklerville, NJ. She typically writes poetry, and dystopian, fantasy, and horror fiction. This is her fifth traditional publication, though she has self-published her own zines, and received a First Place Denise Gess Literary Award for Fiction as well. Her Instagram handle is @lanitwriting, and her website is https://lanit593.wixsite.com/lanitwriting.

My Dear Dad

Dear Dad,

I love you.

Just thought I'd get that out of the way—

This won't be as silly as you sometimes are.

My dearest father, oh how much you do—

Working such long hours, so much stress

Coming home and smiling at us,

As if your day wasn't hard or tiring,

As if you weren't carrying our family on your back.

I worry about you, as most daughters do—

You're my only dad, and I don't want you to

be so drained all the time.

I want you to be happy, relaxed, and hopeful,

I want you to be silly, and full of laughter,

I want to show you the stars,

See your world light up with the youthful

innocence you sacrificed for us.

I want to see the dreams you've

relinquished return to you,

I want to see you flourish and do

what makes your heart *sing*,

I want the life you've given us to

also be spread to you.

My dearest father, oh how much you do—

I cannot buy you much,

I have very little in that regard,

I can't help you with your job,

I do not have the qualifications like you do,

I cannot take your burdens on as my own,

though I'd love to lift the weight from your shoulders.

If I *could*, I would become Atlas, just as you have for us—

You've given me so much,

but I have so little that I can give back to you.

My dearest father, oh how much you do,

You showed me the moon,

and taught me to reach for the stars,

You've handed me the tools to carve

my place in this world,

You've given me solace where I could find none—

So many wonderful things you do

A lifetime isn't long enough to return it to you,

Nor is it enough to spend with you.

My dearest father, oh how much I love you

Though I am small, you taught me to dream big

So with all the strength you've instilled in me,

I will do my best to honor you,

And become the woman you've raised me to be.

With a role model so great, I could never fail,

So I write this poem to you, for you,

I love you.

My dearest father, I'd give the world for you.

Victor Hugo Mendevil is an emerging poet and literary scholar based in Boston. Originally from Seattle, he holds an MFA in Creative Writing from Hofstra University and is pursuing his PhD in English at Northeastern University — where he currently teaches collegiate writing. Victor has received fellowships from Eckerd College's Writers in Paradise Conference (St. Petersburg, FL) and DISQUIET's International Literary Program (Lisbon, Portugal), and was shortlisted for the 2025 DISQUIET Literary Prize in Poetry. His most recent published work may be read, or is forthcoming, in *The Malahat Review, Fourteen Hills, ANMLY,*

Pangyrus LitMag, Harbor Review, In the Time & Life Of anthology (City of Boston), and *America's Best Emerging Poets* (Z Publishing). He can be discovered on Instagram @victorhugomendevil.

A Family Man

We were all working little Amazon jobs back then.

We acted like a pandemic was a draft –

then, a bullet.

It wasn't until we cried about it

that we realized we could not survive this war of

infection and household payments,

the jobs were lost

the hangovers hanging over

typed-out gaming codes, headphones on,

ignoring what's outside.

That was the case

until I took the headphones off one night:

in the slits, I could see him

getting prepared for work at three am.

I see him, still, all these years later:

pulling his pants up, sucking in his stomach,

clicking everything into place for us.

Erik Peters is a father and avid mediaevalist from Vancouver, Canada. His writing is influenced by late antiquity, his family, and his students. Erik has been featured in Coffin Bell, Zoetic, Takahe, Beyond Literary Words, and Thirty West. You can check out all Erik's work at erikpeters.ca.

Braided

In you, we are braided
woven by an unseen hand
whose deftness whorls and warps
a thread so fine
no needle could disturb its helixed plait.

Hours pass
in tracing stitchwork through your flesh
in guessing at the spool
that gave itself to form your knit.

We have our runners, pillings, tears;
patches whose cunning intimacy shows;
stains and rips within our helixed plait
all to show old skins ill-suit new wine.

But you,
in you
the Weaver has renewed
the dye and loomwork
we have worn
so long.

Maureen Martinez (she/her) is a late-blooming,
emerging writer and irreverent woman of faith
working at an all-boys Catholic high school in New
York City for over 20 years. She comes from a long
line of pine tree ramblers, blood moon dancers and
raucous storytellers, which explains a lot. Her work
is published or forthcoming in *Gramercy Review,*
Folly Journal, Boudin, Prime Number Magazine,
Washington Square Review, Meniscus, BAR BAR,
Artemis, Broadkill Review, Unwoven Literary
Magazine and others.

Getting the Ju-Ju Out

WAIT! You gotta get the Ju-Ju out first.

My husband says as we make the bed together

in our two bedroom apartment on Centre Avenue.

Ok I guess, I said. *But WHAT??* A thought I kept

to myself amused but annoyed because I had shit to
get

done and this was taking too long for a mother of
four

and it was Saturday, one of two days off, and I
wanted

to have some rest time and down time and time

for *MYSELF. Is that too much to ask for?*

But he went on sweeping the sheets back and forth

in what appeared to be a ritual of sorts while making

rhythmic tribal sounds—

Ding-ga-da   Ding-ga-da   Ding-ga-da

Are we good? I asked through clenched teeth

and a sarcastic tone. *Yeah,* he said. *We're good.*

We've been together 27 years now, so I concede

there's something to it. Thus my advice to my sons

when they find the one is this:

Before you sleep and when you wake up take time

to sweep the sheets together. Because marriage is
tough

and life is short and the bad Ju-Ju's gotta get out.

And don't forget about the *Ding-ga-das*.

Tetiana Yatsechko-Blazhenko is a writer from Ukraine. She holds a Master's degree in History. She has published books, poetry, and short stories, including *Museum Sociology: Presentation in Space and Time* (co-authored). Her work appears in literary journals such as *Foxylit* and *Indigo*, and in anthologies including *Shepit Sester* and *Koromyslo*. She won the 2025 "Odesa Miniature" contest and placed second in the 2025 "Chuhuiv Miniature" contest.

Reverence

In my veins flows the blood of my grandfathers –
Warriors and farmers,
They passed down to me
A love for life and the land.
Their lives were shaped by wars and repression.
They endured,
Rising from the depths.
They built a life from nothing,
Each one built a home from ruins.
Each one learned to value the grain,
For they survived hunger.
I stand by their graves
And break the bread, as they did,
from the wheat of their fields.
Today, their sons have gone
To defend the land from enemies.
Today, their descendants need
The warrior's blood in their veins
More than ever before.
This battle will be long,
But truth will prevail.
And grandchildren will come
To place their hands on cold stone, in reverence.

Joris Soeding's most recent collection of poetry is
After Highland Park (Origami Poems Project, 2021).
Soeding's writing has appeared in publications such
as *Another Chicago Magazine*, *Poetry Pacific*,
Portage Magazine, and *Tint Journal*. He is a
fifth/sixth grade Social Studies teacher in Chicago,
where he resides with his family.

Casa Lupita

year after year we celebrated my birthday there

my favorite restaurant and family preferred

surprises when I was little

mami and papa would blindfold me in the backseat

alter the route for a fifteen-minute drive

eyes covered until the door

mami explaining to passersby

outside the songs of Mexico—I knew where we were

tiled and stuccoed, archways,

tables around a fountain and natural light

mami and I would laugh when papa excused himself

citing the restroom but really

announced my birthday to the waitress

I acted surprised but was ecstatic

with singing from servers

fried ice cream in caramel with chatter

of families just before Christmas

Amari Murray (she/her) is a poet from Brooklyn, New York. She holds a B.A. in Creative Writing from Purchase College, SUNY. She began writing poetry at the age of eight, later publishing her first poem, "Prayers For The Fear of Family Pandemics", in high school. Her work explores secrets, self-discovery, and survival through vivid imagery, layered emotion, and lyrical rhythm. When she writes, it is drawn from her personal experiences, rooted in the dualities of pleasure and pain, silence and voice, intimacy and independence. She has performed at the Bowery Poetry Club and Girls Write Now. As well as her work having appeared in the *Consortium COVID-19 Journal*, she has an upcoming publication in the *Spoken Black Girl Magazine* in February 2026.

Not by Blood,
But by Heart

He didn't arrive

with a script,

just patience.

No promises,

expectations,

only time.

First,

I kept my distance,

unsure how to trust a man

who wasn't there

from the beginning.

But he never asked me

to call him anything

he just listened,

and showed up again.

He taught me

care isn't always loud,

it can exist

in the everyday

the rides home,

the small check-ins,

the way he made sure

I was seen

when I tried to disappear.

He guided me gently,

through the rough edges

of adulthood

not by fixing me,

but reminding me

I wasn't broken.

When I look at him now,

I see a relationship

not bound by blood,

but built from trust.

Justin Marlowe is an author who currently lives in Fredericksburg, Virginia. After embarking on a career as a writer, he's been fortunate enough to have his memoir, _Perfect Strangers: Echoes of a Black Suburban Youth_, published, as well as five of his poems; one within the World Poetry Collective's, _Poets of a New Generation_ compilation, two within the BIPOC centered Literary magazine, _Alma Lit_, and one with the UK's, _The Lost Letter Project_, and another with Glass Gates Publishing. While building a solid portfolio of published work is never easy in such a competitive industry, Justin is on a fast track toward success and notoriety.

Nature's Morphine

A patriarchal denial;

Facetiously dismissive and cavalier.

Bet you can't keep pace for three miles...

At eight years of age, one recognized the

assignment to be instantaneously obligatory.

Triumph was unquestionably essential

for my welfare.

As a tandem, a trek was embarked

upon en route toward a southern dirt track.

Shrubs, weeds, and undergrowth in dank prosperity.

Revolting, but functional.

Oppressive humidity had been released

into an engulfing frenzy of consumption.

A resting respiratory rate was unfeasible.

Nonetheless, push forward and cease to yield.

The event commenced with a dozen laps

versus a robust adult.

The brain assembled for combat.

Just complete the task. Fulfill the manufactured void.

Glide at a suitable pace...

Execute accordingly; perform within yourself.

Done! But what shall be the result?

The adrenaline was the plug

and the endorphins came from the dealer.

A patriarchal denial;

Manifesting a byproduct greater than

the sum of its parts.

Nature's morphine.

An intoxicant with an efficacious result.

Much obliged, father.

Plausible deniability at its finest.

You may be ethereal in spirit,

but your shadow is both pervasive and present.

Lessons absorbed from the dealer.

Push forward and cease to yield.

John Robinson is a mainstream, Appalachian-American poet and scholar from the Kanawha Valley in Mason County, West Virginia. His 182 literary works have appeared in 127 journals and presses throughout the United States, Australia, Canada, the United Kingdom, India, Poland, Germany and China. His first chapbook, _June's Fisher of Solitudes_, was published with Mountain State Press in March of 2025. He is also a published printmaker with 104 art images and photographs appearing in forty-two journals, electronic and print, in the United States, Italy, Ireland and the United Kingdom. Recent Literary Work; _Poet's Choice Anthology: Elegy, Ulu_

Review, *Literary Yard*, *Language and Semiotic Studies*, *Origami Poets Project*, *Periodicities: A Journal of Poetry and Poetics*, *Mountain State Press*, *The Wallace Stevens Journal* and *Critical Survey*.

Baling Hay

—for Lucas Wayne

I remember days when sweat

would run from my face,

soak my shirt, lifting and throwing

those light, ripe and heavy, green,

aromatic bales.

My father would stop and stack the wagon,

and in the barn he placed them

cut side down for curing.

Where would your voice fall

among the leaves?

Would you breathe the still, hot air

of an August afternoon?

Would you game it up in air conditioning,

or bury your nose in a cell phone?

Would you love the feel of dirt on your hands,

your life just as full of promise?

Would you set tobacco with the rest of us

and laugh with dad at how little all that

sweat and labor ever brought?

Would you walk with that little ghost

and be inseparable,

guardian of a being who never was,

though we know existed,

whose nature was androgynous,

whose life was forming just as yours

or mine?

Lucas Wayne would have been the hunter,

closer to the earth,

a truer balance, maybe.

I could never stomach all the gore of killing,

that putrid smell,

my father's blood-smeared hands,

steam rising from the deer's body,

those eyes empty of all life,

cast as clouded marble.

previously published in Blue Collar Review 2018

Martina Madden is an Irish writer from East Cork. She works in the heritage and museum sector surrounded by the richness of art, history, beautiful things and gardens. She writes about ordinary everyday things, family and the people and places that are most important to her. Publishing success is relatively new having first been published early in 2025.

The Morning Of....

When I came in from the short hallway

dressed in satin, pearls, and hairspray,

your face said enough.

Momentous words were neither whispered,

nor shared with our audience in the living room,

while the photographer fumbled

with and tested another lens.

The hold of your hand over mine

guarded a palpable love, kept me.

You gulped air in anxious breaths

and failed your rehearsed speech.

Your thumb brushed your chin.

A tremble in that nervous of ticks.

These things, so simply shown,

said enough and were on their own,

momentous.

Tim Boardman is a poet based in West Yorkshire whose work explores the quiet beauty of everyday life, the shifting landscapes of the North, and the complexities of human connection. Drawing inspiration from nature, memory, and local heritage, his poems are both grounded and lyrical, often balancing emotional honesty with wry observation. His writing has been featured in local readings, community arts projects, and online literary platforms. Tim's commitment to accessible, resonant poetry has made him a distinctive voice within the regional arts scene.

Inheritance

I'm rubbing

my hands again —

some insect's bitten me, I think.

It itches.

It was a Dad thing,

the way he rubbed his hands —

absently, endlessly —

a flicker of routine

in a world unfastening.

I thought it was

repetitive behaviour

or just

old age.

It's strangely

soothing

and disturbing.

Now I feel it

under my own skin:

that ritual,

that need

to soothe

something unseen.

I look down —

liver spots bloom

like small bruises.

My hands

have become his.

I rub

as if remembering

Erick Phillips Garske is a poet, spoken word artist, father, and the author of a full-length collection of poetry, *Words Alone*. He is a Pushcart Prize nominee. He lives in southern California with a young dog, a Cavalier, and near his two young adult sons.

Father and Son

For Alan

lacing your shoestrings
into makeshift rabbit ears
as a toddler is the one memory
that ties this moment
together
as you graduate in your cap and gown
to your past
as a I tie your shoe
and take care of
these final loose ends

Mark Andrew Heathcote is an adult learning
difficulties support worker. His poems have been
published in journals, magazines, and anthologies
online and in print. He is from Manchester and
resides in the UK. Mark is the author of *In Perpetuity*
and *Back on Earth*, two books of poems published by
Creative Talents Unleashed.

A man carries an icon hand-painted

A man carries an icon in his heart and more

He crosses the steppes in search of a distant shore.

He's a wanderer, a rambler, lain up feeling lame

He goes to the end of the world to exclaim.

And proclaim he's got only one home!

He goes to the sea white, watery, milky foam

To transcend loss every step, and find salvation.

He sees devils and saints under trackless skies

The sores on his soles bleed, his heart's in flotation

Like a dove, it soars.

Every step needs still to synchronize.

He goes on and on, on and on, amen!

His own heart, his best friend,

an icon hand-painted, amen.

This man is on his way

This man doesn't need honey or jam

Or syrup from a can.

This man doesn't need a thankless job

Or a till register to rob.

This man doesn't need a loveless marriage

He's got big ideas and plenty of courage.

This man knows his ultimate true calling

And isn't afraid of leaping and falling.

This man is on his way; he's a sure success

If he knows just what it takes and what to re-address

This man is a star, a Phoenix rising.

He isn't any longer self-loathing

Or the least-bit self-despising.

This man is humble, and he's thankful for-all-he's-got

And all the tribulations he was allotted.

This man walks tall beside me; he is my true destiny,

He sits lowly beside me, deputies my future self.

Also, he says he does honestly love me.

This man reminds me to be always thankful

This man is me if I choose him to be

With much improved better health

And a world-of-endless wealth.

This man is me if I just will him to be.

About Us

Quillkeepers Press, LLC is a small indie press and indie author resource group. We publish themed anthologies on a variety of topics, as well as provide resources and services to indie authors. We pride ourselves on the quality of our traditionally published titles, as well as our reasonably priced services for indie authors who prefer to do it themselves. It is a deep passion of ours to help as many writers' voices as possible be heard. As indie artists ourselves, we understand most creatives operate within a strict budget. Therefore, it has always been a priority of ours to keep our rates reasonable. Our corporate climate is not one of profit but one of helping bring dreams to fruition. Our motto sums it up best: *"Reading between the lines, to make your words take flight"*.

We produce between 3 and 6 anthologies annually. We don't charge artists to be published in our anthologies, although tips are welcome through Submittable.com to cover the cost of the ad space, ISBN number registration, copyright fees, as well as other overhead costs.

As writers ourselves, we understand how challenging the market can be and how difficult it is to get work into the hands of a larger audience. Therefore, we accept and encourage our contributors to submit both new and previously published compositions (as long as the previous publisher allows it). Too often, we find publishers who want exclusive rights to the work being published. This is counterproductive if the artist wants their message to reach as many people as possible. Having been in and studied the industry for years, our founder has concluded that many writers take great pride in their work and produce it for their own healing.

Furthermore, they share said work, hoping it helps others heal. For all the aforementioned reasons, it is our current policy to request non-exclusive rights to our contributors' work rather than exclusive rights. In essence, our artists are allowing us to borrow their prized writing, and we are incredibly grateful.

It is also for those same reasons that we consider ourselves an indie publishing services company, rather than a traditional publisher. Traditional publishing typically involves a lengthy contract, exclusive rights to work, and royalties. We would rather help wrap artists' products into a beautiful package and allow them to set their own parameters, price points, and keep all their royalties from sales.

On a final note, whether you have employed our services or lent us your voice in an anthology, thank you for entrusting us with your craft. If you would like to participate in a forthcoming anthology, please check out our Submittable page at www.submittable.com. For more information on our services, please visit our website www.quillkeeperspress.com

Keep the quill moving,

Stephanie Lamb, Founder, EIC

Quillkeepers Press, LLC

Other Books Produced by Quillkeepers Press

Soon, A New Day

A rise of the Phoenix-themed anthology of essays, memoirs, short stories, and poetry by various artist

Turning Dark into Light and Other Magic Tricks of the Mind

A mental health-themed anthology of essays, memoirs, short stories, and poetry by various artists

Rearing in the Rearview

A parenting-themed anthology of essays, memoirs, short stories, and poetry by various artists

Verbal Vomit and Other Poetry and Prose

A poetry and prose collection by Stephanie Lamb

Tan Lines

A Summer Solstice-inspired anthology of memoirs, short stories, and poetry by various artists.

Bare Bones

A Halloween-inspired anthology of essays, memoirs, short stories, and poetry by various artists.

Snowdrifts

A Winter Solstice-inspired anthology of essays, memoirs, short stories, and poetry by various artists.

Sapling

A Spring equinox-inspired anthology of essays, memoirs, short stories, and poetry by various artists.

Dislocated

The debut poetry collection by Dylan Webster.

Botany of Gaia

A nature-inspired anthology of essays, memoirs, short stories, and poetry by various artists.

Harvest

A Fall equinox-inspired anthology of essays, memoirs, short stories, and poetry by various artists.

The Matador's Wife

A chapbook-length collection of poetry by Andrés Colón.

scars & lyres

A chapbook-length collection of poetry by ww harris.

Inspired

An art-inspired-by-art anthology of essays, memoirs, short stories, poetry, and artwork.

Smitten

A love-inspired anthology of essays, memoirs, short stories, and poetry.

High Water

A chapbook-length collection of poetry by Carrie Carter.

Notable Moons

A Chapbook-length collection of poetry by David Gunton.

My West

A chapbook-length collection of poetry by Jenifer Fox.

Lightwaves

A YA Historical Fiction novella

AmerAsian

A poetry collection by Kimberly McAfee.

The Savior and the Shadow Queen

A poetry collection by Kimberly McAfee.

Turning the Corner

A poetry collection by Lori Ulrich.

Purge & Bloom

A chapbook-length poetry collection by Brooks Decker.

Arranging Words

A chapbook-length poetry collection by Fran Abrams.

__Words for Women__

A chapbook-length poetry collection by Lori Heninger.

__Lent Words__

A chapbook-length poetry collection by Christine Moore.

__Talking to Ghosts__

A chapbook-length poetry collection by Jon Tobias.

__A House with Bad Bones__

A poetry collection by Adeline Tatum

__The Wake of the Hound Dogs__

A witty must-read novel by AD Matson

__Alchemies, Arrivals__

An eco-poetry chapbook collection by Sophia Pinto Thomas

__Ikusei: Nurture__

A carefully curated anthology of haikus by various authors.

**Weaving the Light**

A women's appreciation anthology from voices
across the globe.

**Interbeing**

A chapbook-length poetry collection by Soraya
Bakhbakhi

**The House as Witness**

A chapbook-length poetry collection by Veronica
Tucker